Herbal Vinegar

Maggie Oster

A STOREY PUBLISHING BOOK

STOREY

Storey Communications, Inc.
Schoolhouse Road
Pownal, Vermont 05261

For Sueann
May she always wear her hat well
and dance to her heart's content.

——————

Edited by Lorin Driggs and Gwen Steege
Cover and text design by Leslie Morris Noyes
Production by Kevin L. Harvey
Cover photograph by A. Blake Gardner
Vinegars by Goat Rock Vinegars, Bennington, Vermont
Line drawings by Brigita Fuhrmann and Charles Joslin
Indexed by Northwind Editorial Services

Printed in the United States by Book Press
Third Printing, October 1994

Library of Congress Cataloging-in-Publication Data

Oster, Maggie
      Herbal vinegar / Maggie Oster.
              p.   cm.
      Includes bibliographical references (p.   ) and index.
           ISBN 0-88266-876-5 (hc) — ISBN 0-88266-843-9 (pb)
           1. Cookery (Vinegar)   I. Title.
      TX819.V5084   1994
      641.6'22—dc20   93-20858

Contents

SOME THOUGHTS ABOUT VINEGAR

Some of life's most worthwhile lessons are learned in the simplest of ways. For example, my appreciation of vinegar came not from savoring rare, imported vinegars sprinkled on mâche and radicchio in restaurants, but rather from my thrifty mother, who used the vinegar left from a jar of homemade pickles as a dressing on just-picked, home-grown Bibb lettuce. And don't make fun until you've had my mother's salad dressing! Of course, the taste does vary, depending on the particular preserved food that just vacated the jar. That's precisely why I learned at an early age to appreciate the nuances of flavors possible in vinegars.

Obviously, my family did not live frivolously, and store-bought vinegars consisted strictly of the distilled and cider varieties. Even with these, certain miracles were wrought on meats, vegetables, and fruits. My father made pickled tongue without peer, and leftover beets were no secondary fare when they made a return appearance in a vinegar sauce.

Only later in life, while haunting the aisles of Macy's and Balducci's in New York, did I discover that vinegars could be made or flavored with all sorts of exotic ingredients, such as raspberry, tarragon, sherry, honey, rice, malt, and various wines, including champagne. The potential uses of vinegars in cooking multiplied before my eyes.

I bought, smelled, tasted, admired the colors, and considered the complexities and subtleties of the many vinegars I discovered. Then, I began learning how to use them in soups, marinades, even drinks. The piquant, tantalizing tastes added new flavor to salads, vegetables, main courses, and desserts. Pickles and relishes took on fresh personalities, too.

Although I have been involved in gardening much of my life, it was only some twenty years ago that I became interested in growing herbs. Eventually, I was growing hundreds of different ones. I read books about herbs and found all kinds of suggestions and recipes for herb vinegars. I started trying different combinations, using ideas from the books and developing my own.

How wonderful to discover that I could make so many vinegars at home. Purple basil, garlic chives, rose petal, fennel, chive blossom, and elder flower were just a few of the possibilities. Plus, there were blends of herbs and spices. The

1

colors, too, were beautiful. Jars of homemade vinegar filled my shelves. Soon I was sharing vinegars with friends, giving them as gifts and making them for the local herb society to sell.

As my interest and curiosity grew, I read more and more about the history, types, and uses of vinegars. This book is the result of my research. Here's a summary of just what it offers you.

Chapter 1 presents a brief history of vinegar, from what is known about its ancient origins to its many varieties and uses through the centuries up to the present day. Next, in Chapter 2 there's a discussion of the many kinds of vinegars available in stores and by mail order, including a description of flavors and general suggestions for using the different varieties. You'll also find step-by-step directions for making wine vinegars at home and for flavoring store-bought vinegars with herbs, flowers, fruits, spices, and vegetables. Besides individual flavors, there are also recipes for combinations of ingredients. All of these homemade vinegars are very inexpensive and easy to make. Included are suggestions of ways to bottle your vinegars and decorate for gift-giving.

If you've always wanted to grow your own herbs for flavoring vinegars, Chapter 3 provides easily followed, concise information for growing the best "vinegar herbs." Even if you don't have garden space, many of these herbs are readily grown in containers on a patio or deck, or even indoors.

No book about vinegar would be complete without a description of the many household, health, and beauty uses for this versatile liquid. Chapter 4 contains hundreds of "recipes" for using the inexpensive distilled or cider vinegars as well as specially scented ones. These will save you time and money (and will fascinate you as well). Whether for cleaning carpets, bottles, laundry, the shower, or your face, vinegar could be the solution for you.

The heart of this book is Part II, containing more than 175 recipes in which vinegar is an ingredient. Whether you already have a pantry shelf filled with dozens of vinegars or you're just getting interested, these recipes will help you discover the many opportunities for cooking with vinegar. Using vinegar in cooking often reduces calories and the amount of salt in foods while adding a bracing tang and penetrating complexity of flavor. Included are recipes for appetizers, main courses, soups, pastas, grains, dry beans, vegetables, dressings, marinades, sauces and salsas, mustards, ketchups, pickles, relishes, other preserved foods, jellies, jams, desserts, and candies. A comprehensive sources section lists mail-order suppliers of vinegars, vinegar-making kits, bottles, labels, and herb seeds and plants. Finally, there's a selected list that suggests further reading about vinegars, herb-growing, and cooking.

I've always dearly loved eating, and I can't remember a time in my life when I didn't enjoy salads, pickles, and other foods flavored with vinegar. The past years — in which I have made, used, doused, splashed, scrubbed, and endlessly experimented with vinegar — have been a marvelous period of fascination and discovery. I sincerely hope that, with this book, I can share with you at least some of my own enthusiasm for the many possibilities of vinegar.

A Brief History
of Vinegar

The origin of vinegar is one of those fortunate happenstances never specifically noted in any historical record. Among the oldest of foods and medicine known to humans, its discovery most likely occurred sometime about ten thousand years ago, concurrent with the advent of wine, since vinegar is the natural next step after alcoholic fermentation. California winemaker August Sebastiani has been quoted as saying, "God is trying to make vinegar. It is the winemaker's job to stay his hand." In the centuries before wine production was perfected, much of the wine inevitably became vinegar. In fact, the French wine port of Orléans became known for its vinegar in the fourteenth century because of the frequency of this occurrence.

The earliest written references acknowledge wine and vinegar made from dates being commonplace as a medicine in Babylonia, circa 5,000 B.C. Grapes, figs, and other Mediterranean fruits also provided the fermentable substances from which various vinegars were made. There is evidence of Aryan and other nomadic tribes in northern Europe and Asia utilizing apples to make a soured fermented drink. Over the next several thousand years, vinegar's use spread through the Phoenicians, Egyptians, Greeks, Romans, and, hence, to the rest of the Western world.

Along the way a variety of applications evolved for this remarkable liquid, and vinegar soon became indispensable as a means of enhancing the flavor of foods and as preservative for them as well as a curative and cosmetic. Before the advent of modern technology, vinegar, in addition to salt brine, was a major way of preserving food. The acidic nature of vinegar slows down the growth of harmful bacteria in foods.

The ancient Greeks and Romans are known to have kept quantities of vinegar in their cellars, particularly prizing Egyptian vinegar. They used vinegar for cooking — steeping vegetables and marinating meat to tenderize and add flavor, making pickles, and preserving herbs, flowers, and vegetables in vinegar. Sweet-and-sour dishes, especially meat cooked in honey and vinegar and fruits and vegetables preserved in vinegar, were enjoyed in other ancient civilizations.

Bowls filled with vinegar were placed on the tables for dipping bread during meals, a use mentioned in the Old Testament in the Book of Ruth, where it is noted that the reapers soaked their bread in vinegar to freshen it. Vinegar is mentioned in the Bible almost as many times as wine. There is even a specific printing of the Bible that is known as the Vinegar Bible. An Oxford printing of 1716 by John Baskett, the King's printer, was so called because the Parable of the Vineyard (Luke 20: 9–18) was printed as the Parable of the Vinegar.

By the thirteenth century, a wide selection of vinegars — including those flavored with clove, chicory, fennel, ginger, truffle, raspberry, mustard, and garlic —was commonly sold by street vendors in Paris. Pepper vinegar was especially popular during the Middle Ages because wine that contained pepper was not taxed on importation into Paris. Wealthy French cooks in the Middle Ages went to the *saucier*—the vinegar maker for sauces— and seasonings made of vinegar, mustard, herbs, and spices.

Vinegar as a beverage has a long history, too. It is even claimed as part of the reason for the success of the Roman army. Spartianus, a Latin historian, wrote that vinegar mixed with water was the drink of soldiers. This beverage is credited with helping them survive the rigors of battle as well as the various climates they encountered in Europe, Asia, and Africa. Undiluted vinegar not only proved more portable than wine, but also more invigorating.

Since Biblical times, it was the habit of laborers to add a small amount of wine vinegar to water, perhaps with a little salt. This early version of Gatorade, along with some bread, sustained people during their grueling field work under the burning sun. In the United States in the eighteenth and nineteenth centuries, drinks combining fruit juice or water and fruit-flavored vinegar came to be known as "shrubs" or "switchels." These, too, were used by laborers for refreshment during haying and harvesting.

Vinegar has done duty through the ages as a medicine for both external and internal ailments and as a disinfectant and cleanser. Ancient Persian physicians suggested a mixture of lime juice, verjuice (the sour juice of certain fruits), and vinegar to prevent fat accumulation in the body. Early Greek, Roman, and Asian physicians attributed many salutary qualities to vinegar, including aiding digestion, preventing scurvy, and lowering bile levels. Hippocrates, known as the father of

Four Thieves Vinegar

Among all the therapeutic vinegars, Four Thieves Vinegar is legendary. Folklore holds that during one of the plague epidemics in Marseilles, four robbers were able to steal from the dead and dying without themselves succumbing by dousing themselves with this mixture. Recipes vary, but the generally accepted ingredients include the leaves of rosemary, rue, sage, wormwood, and mint plus lavender flowers and camphor gum. Other ingredients sometimes mentioned are calamus root, cinnamon, cloves, nutmeg, and garlic.

medicine, prescribed vinegar to his patients. For "feminine disorders," he recommended a mixture of vinegar, honey, and pepper.

Medieval stillrooms yielded vinegars for "unease" of both stomach and brain, with lavender and rosemary vinegars being two of the favored herbal decoctions. During the plagues in the Middle Ages, robbers in Marseilles are said to have protected themselves from infection with the use of a mixture known as Four Thieves Vinegar. To ward off the noxious odors of raw sewage and garbage, genteel people of the seventeenth and eighteenth centuries held vinegar-soaked sponges to their noses. These sponges were carried in small silver boxes called *vinaigrettes* or in special compartments in the heads of walking canes. In the American Civil War, vinegar was administered to counter scurvy. Even as recently as World War I vinegar was an accepted treatment for wounds.

Modern laboratory analysis verifies the antibacterial and antiseptic properties of vinegar. Many of these uses are just as applicable now, adding yet another dimension to the possibilities of vinegar. A staple of modern self-help medicine is the 1958 book *Folk Medicine* (New York: Holt, Rinehart and Winston) by D. C. Jarvis, M.D., which identifies a number of medicinal uses of apple cider vinegar. From Japan, comes *Rice Vinegar: An Oriental Home Remedy* (Tokyo: Kenko Igakusha Co., 1977) by Togo, Kuroiwa [sic].

Vinegar is also well-ensconced as an interesting footnote to historical figures. Pliny writes that Cleopatra won a wager that she could consume a phenomenally expensive meal by dissolving pearls in vinegar and drinking the result. Hannibal made military use of vinegar by combining it with fire to splinter rocks and facilitate his army's descent of the Alps. The Duc de Meilleraye, grand master of the artillery under Louis XIII, charged the government 1,300,000 francs for vinegar to cool his cannons.

THE NATURAL HISTORY OF VINEGAR

So what exactly is this wonderful, diverse liquid with such a long history and so many uses? Most simply, vinegar is a sour or sharp-tasting liquid containing acetic acid. It is produced from the fermentation of the juice of various fruits or berries, or from honey, molasses, or even from cereal grains as in malt vinegars. Each of these substances imparts its own unique flavor, color, and odor to the final product.

The process of making vinegar begins when fermentation changes the sugars in the material into alcohol and carbonic gas. The gas then evaporates, leaving only the alcohol and the flavors, or esters. In the final phase, oxidation occurs, in which oxygen in the air combines with the alcohol. This is why vinegar forms only when a bottle of wine is uncorked and exposed to air. When alcohol and oxygen combine with the help of a specialized group of microscopic organisms, known as acetobacters, the result is vinegar. The microscopic organisms, mainly various bacteria, form a gelatinous mass known as mother of vinegar.

The old-fashioned way to make vinegar is a slow, natural process. It can take up to several years, depending on the temperature and air circulation. Crocks or glass bottles are used, or even wooden casks as in making fine wine or whiskey. The alcohol comes into contact gradually with air. As it does, it changes into acetic acid, or vinegar, which is heavier than alcohol and slowly sinks to the bottom of the container. Over time, all the alcohol rises to the top and is converted into vinegar.

Modern technology has, of course, speeded up this process. The fermented liquid circulates through large vats, incorporating lots of air and efficiently producing a homogeneous product. These quickly processed vinegars effectively serve as a base to make wonderfully flavored vinegars at home. They are filtered and pasteurized, leaving them sparkling clear. Better-quality aged wine, cider, or malt vinegars are often left unfiltered and unpasteurized, in which cases the bacteria, or mother, will form at the top and sometimes sink to the bottom. This can be used to make your own vinegars, much as sourdough starter is used.

Vinegar can be found in approximately 98 percent of American homes. Until recent years consumption was static and mainly limited to cider and distilled vinegars. With increased interest in the many different kinds and flavors of vinegar over the last several decades, sales have risen 10 percent. The acidity and nutrient content of these vinegars varies. By law in the United States, vinegar must be of at least 4 percent acidity, or 4 grams of acetic acid per 100 cubic centimeters. Other countries have different legal minimums for acidity. Sometimes the acidity is specified by the term *grain,* which refers to the amount of water dilution. A 40-grain vinegar is 4 percent acetic acid.

Low in calories and carbohydrates, vinegar is also low in nutrients. It contains no vitamins, and only small amounts of calcium, phosphorus, iron, and potassium. A cup of cider vinegar is 98.8 percent water, has 34 calories, a trace of protein, no fat, 14.2 grams of carbohydrate, 14 milligrams of calcium, 22 milligrams of phosophorus, 1.4 milligrams of iron, and 2 milligrams of sodium. The most appreciable mineral in apple cider vinegar is potassium at 240 milligrams, while distilled white vinegar has only 36 milligrams of potassium.

Vinegar has been around for thousands of years, and has been taken for granted much of that time. The renaissance of vinegar today stems from its significance as a culinary ingredient and its naturalness for household and personal use. With many forms and uses, vinegar provides us with an opportunity to enliven and enhance our favorite foods, allowing us to develop a healthier cuisine, as well as improve our homes and lives.

WHAT'S IN A NAME

The name vinegar is most often described as being derived from the French words for "sour wine," or vinaigre. But tracing aigre back to the Old French, its meaning was "eager," "sharp," or "biting," while the Latin acer also meant "sharp." This indicates that vinegar's naming may possibly have originally meant "sharp wine" rather than "sour."

BUYING, MAKING, AND FLAVORING VINEGAR

Commercially available vinegars are by no means a recent phenomenon. There are indications that early Mediterranean civilizations were extensively producing vinegars for sale 4,000 years ago, but also commonly flavoring them with herbs, spices, and fruit. For much of the twentieth century, we in the United States have had to make do with far fewer choices. Distilled white, cider, and cider-lookalike vinegars were the major alternatives available to consumers in the U.S. for much of this century, but that has changed radically in the last several decades.

Today, grocery store shelves in almost every community are stocked, at the very least, with red and white wine vinegars in addition to the more mundane varieties. Cosmopolitan areas, with their gourmet, health, and ethnic food shops, offer a wide range of vinegars made from a variety of wines, fruits, and grains. Most of these shops also have vinegars flavored with herbs and fruits. Unfortunately, many of the vinegars are often not only overpriced, but made from distilled or lesser quality wine vinegars.

Flavoring vinegars is among the easiest of gardening crafts, and the combinations you can create are limited only by your imagination. A challenge facing anyone who wants to create flavored vinegars comes in choosing the vinegar with which to start. The quality of vinegars available varies greatly, depending on the method of production. The only sure way to tell the quality is by tasting and comparing. Do the quality and flavor of the vinegar you buy really matter when you are going to flavor it at home with herbs, spices, flowers, and fruit? To a great extent, yes, although this doesn't mean you must buy a premium vinegar. A medium-price vinegar is usually of sufficient character to make a good flavored vinegar. Many people prefer vinegars that are made from organic sources or that are unfiltered and unpasteurized, as more care and attention often go into the manufacturing process. The advantages of pasteurizing are that bacterial activity is curtailed and quality is more consistent.

Vinegar Tasting

One way of determining which vinegars you prefer, as well as which ones will go best with different herbs or other flavorings, is to have a vinegar tasting. This can be as simple or as elaborate as you desire. The one key difference from a wine tasting is that it is more difficult to keep the taste buds open when sampling vinegars. As a general rule, you should taste no more than five or six at a time.

To taste vinegar, drink it straight, diluted, or on sugar cubes. Whichever method you choose, give your taste buds a break between samples with unsalted crackers or bread and plain mineral water.

If you are tasting a vinegar straight, just pour a small amount in a wine glass, hold it up to the light and look at it, smell it, and take a little sip. Let it stay in your mouth for a few seconds before swallowing slowly. To dilute vinegar for tasting, combine 1 teaspoon of vinegar with 2 tablespoons of plain bottled water. To taste from a sugar cube, use a slow-dissolving, rectangular cube. Briefly dip an end of the cube into the vinegar, then gently suck out the vinegar. Use a fresh cube for each vinegar tasted.

Unless a vinegar is unfiltered, it should be clear. Good vinegars have a clean aroma that is not too strong, and a pleasing, full taste. The best vinegars have an intricacy of flavor and aroma that is rich, smooth, and subtle. The aftertaste should be subtle and pleasant rather than harsh or biting.

Commercial Vinegar Production

In the Western world, commercial vinegar production was formally established in Orléans, France, with the French guild of professional vinegar makers, the *Corporatif des Maîtres-Vinaigriers d'Orléans,* in 1394. The importance of this group is indicated by the fact that the best vinegars are still made by the "Orléans process." Also called the slow process, this method involves combining wine and unpasteurized vinegar with vinegar bacteria in wooden barrels or vats. The wine is slowly changed to acetic acid over a period of at least one to six months. The process is slow because only a relatively small amount of wine is exposed to air at any time. As vinegar is formed it sinks to the bottom of the container and is drawn off, while the wine remains at the top, exposed to air and the vinegar bacteria. The temperature is maintained at 70° F so none of the flavor esters in the wine or other liquid is lost.

In the 1700s, the Dutch physician Herman Boerhaave developed a quicker process that involved packing larger casks with grape pomace. In 1835, a German named J. S. Schutzenback elaborated on Boerhaave's method. Known as the German, generator, or quick process, it involves the use of a large two-chambered fermenting vessel, or generator. The upper chamber is filled with bacteria-inoculated wood shavings, corncobs, charcoal, chunks of pottery, or other material. Air is blown up through this material as wine or other fermented liquid percolates downward and collects in the lower chamber. The temperature is kept at about 100° F. The liquid is recirculated through the top chamber until all the wine is converted into vinegar, in about a week. The resulting vinegar is aged for several weeks in tanks or barrels, then it is filtered, bottled, and usually pasteurized by heating it to 140° to 150°F. Because heat is used in this process, the most delicate flavors are driven off.

The cheapest way to produce vinegar is the continuous, or submerged fermentation process. A device called a Frings acetator forces air up through the wine or fermented liquid that is held in stainless steel tanks at about 100°F. Vinegar is made in as little as one day. Some manufacturers age it in large wooden tanks prior to filtering, bottling, and pasteurizing.

An A to Z of Vinegars

Many kinds of commercial vinegar are readily available at local supermarkets or ethnic specialty shops, or for mail-order sources, see pages 162–164.

Balsamic Vinegar

Balsamic vinegar is noted for its brown color, intense fruity aroma, and exquisite sweet-and-sour flavor. The most celebrated of all vinegars, the true *aceto balsamico* is seldom available, while the officially sanctioned substitute, commercially available only since 1966, sells for a minor king's ransom— when it can be found. The less-expensive industralized version is widely available.

The true *aceto balsamico* vinegar is produced only in the Emilia-Romagna region of northern Italy that stretches from the Adriatic Sea to within a few miles of the Gulf of Genoa. It has been made since the eleventh century. Highly prized since its earliest days, it was given as a ducal gift to the Holy Roman Emperor Henry III in 1046 as well as to other important European statesmen through the centuries. The name balsamic, from *balsam* and *balm,* is derived from its supposed medicinal properties, including its use as a protection against the plague.

Until recently balsamic vinegar was produced for family use only, with barrels passed from one generation to the next, often aging for fifty to two hundred or more years. It was sometimes even used as part of a dowry. True *aceto balsamico* starts out as must (unfermented juice) from grapes that have a high sugar content, most notably Trebbiano grapes. When it has begun to ferment, it is boiled over a wood fire in copper cauldrons until reduced by at least a third. It is then combined with vinegar containing active bacteria cultures and placed in the first of a series of progressively smaller wooden casks, called *batteria.* The *batteria* may be made of juniper, oak, chestnut, mulberry, cherry, locust, alder, or ash.

Traditionally, this aging process occurs in the attic of the house, with the women of the household responsible for its care, as depicted in thirteenth-century paintings. The alternating heat and cold of the seasons are essential to the slow changes wrought in the vinegar. With an evaporation rate of about 10 percent each year, 100 liters of must will become only 15 liters of vinegar twelve years later. When the flavor is found acceptably intense, the vinegar is sealed in a final small wooden cask.

The officially sanctioned substitute for the true *aceto balsamic* vinegar has an Italian government designation of *Denominazione di origine controllata* (DOC) and is controlled by the Consortium of Producers of the Traditional Balsamic Vinegar of Modena. This vinegar is at least twelve years old, but often twenty to thirty years old, and sells for a hundred dollars or more in 3.3-ounce bottles.

A handful of producers in Modena make a quick-process industrialized balsamic vinegar, which is sold under different labels in the United States. For this version, either the grape juice is caramelized (cooked until it changes color) or caramelized sugar is added and sometimes flavorings, then it is aged in large vats with wood chips for flavor. According to Italian law, for a vinegar to be labeled *aceto balsamico* it must be aged at least three years. It is usually 6 percent acidity.

To maintain its luscious flavor, balsamic vinegar is added at the end of cooking or used as a condiment to enhance the flavors of foods. Some common uses for balsamic vinegar include deglazing a skillet after sautéing liver or chicken, sprinkling it on fresh strawberries, adding it to sparkling mineral water to make a beverage, or using it as an ingredient in salad dressings and marinades for steamed or roasted vegetables or seafood. For a treat, sprinkle some on shaved white truffles with grated Parmigiano-Reggiano and heat just until the cheese melts. Traditionalists sip *aceto balsamico* from tiny liqueur glasses as an after-dinner cordial.

Cane Vinegar

Made from fermented sugar cane extract and water, cane vinegar has a low acidity (4 percent) and is most used in Philippine cooking. Relatively uncommon, it can be most easily found in ethnic groceries.

Champagne Vinegar

Most vinegars labeled as champagne are produced from still dry white wine made from grapes usually used to make champagne, such as Chardonnay or Pinot Noir. Champagne vinegars are made by any of the methods used to create wine vinegars, and have an acidity of 5 to 6 percent. The best champagne vinegars are soft, smooth, and delicate. They go well in sauces with light poultry or seafood dishes. They are excellent vinegars for flavoring with the milder herbs, fruit, and flowers.

Cider Vinegar

Second only to distilled white vinegar in availabilty, cider vinegar has many uses in cooking, from salad dressings to pickling to any dish calling for vinegar. This vinegar has a fruity flavor. For flavoring, cider vinegar is best with medium- or strong-flavored herbs and spices.

The best cider vinegars are made from whole apples ground into pulp, cold-pressed to extract the cider, fermented in wooden barrels, and aged for at least six months for a rich, full flavor. Cheaper kinds are made from apple cores and peelings, then quickly processed. Organic cider vinegars are available at health-food stores and are usually unfiltered. Most are 5 percent acidity. When shopping, beware of "cider" vinegars that are actually caramel-colored distilled vinegar with a small amount of concentrated cider stock added.

Cider vinegar is particularly noted for the medicinal claims made for it, including its ability to maintain general good health, cure arthritis, the common cold, and indigestion, and promote weight loss.

COCONUT VINEGAR

With a distinct musty flavor and unique aftertaste, coconut vinegar has a low acidity (4 percent). It is usually found in ethnic groceries and is most often used with Asian cooking, especially Thai cuisine.

DISTILLED VINEGAR

Made from grain, a petroleum by-product, or wood pulp, distilled vinegar is a harsh, coarse-flavored vinegar that is usually colorless. Most brands are diluted to 5 percent acidity. Distilled vinegar is used widely in the commercial production of pickles and other foods. Home use is best limited to household chores or, perhaps, pickling.

MALT VINEGAR

Essential to English fish and chips, robustly flavored malt vinegar is to cereal grains as wine vinegar is to grapes. Made in England and northern Europe as early as the 1600s as a way to utilize soured beer, malt vinegar was originally called alegar. It is manufactured from malted barley and grain mash that is heated and fermented into a beerlike liquid, then combined with beech, birch, or other wood shavings in large steel or plastic vats that contain vinegar bacteria. Finally, the vinegar is filtered, matured, and colored with caramel. It usually has 5 percent acidity.

Because of its hearty taste, malt vinegar is best when used with the more heavily spiced pickles, chutneys, relishes, ketchups, and mustards. Some people prefer malt vinegar in remoulade and tartar sauces, and the English favor it in mint sauce for roast lamb.

RICE VINEGAR

Made by the Chinese for over 5,000 years, rice vinegar generally has a mild, slightly sweet flavor. Chinese rice vinegar is usually made from rice wine, or sake, and comes in three forms. The kind made from red rice is used as dip for fried foods and steamed crustaceans, and as a condiment in soups, especially shark's fin. White rice vinegar is actually a pale golden color and enhances sweet-and-sour dishes. Rich, bittersweet, and robust, Chinese black vinegar may be made from wheat, millet, or sorghum as well as from rice. Its smoky flavor augments stir-fries and salad dressings.

Called *su*, Japanese rice vinegar is milder, sweeter, and more mellow than the Chinese variety. The manufacturing process is unique in that all the production steps are combined into one. Cooked rice is combined with a fermentation catalyst called *koji,* water, and vinegar bacteria in sunken earthenware jars. Because the grain remains present throughout the fermentation and vinegar-producing process, this rice vinegar has a significant amino acid content. The medical claims made for Japanese rice vinegar include the ability to neutralize lactic acid in the body, alkalinize the blood, and generally promote good health.

There are a number of forms of Japanese rice vinegar. Best known are *aji pon,* which is flavored with citrus juice and soy sauce and used as a meat marinade; *tosazu,* which is flavored with fish stock, sugar, and soy sauce and sprinkled on seafood and vegetables; and *yamabukizu,* a sweet-sour vinegar used for seasoning rice.

In general, rice vinegars are sold at 4 or 5 percent acidity. They combine well with peanut and sesame oils for salad dressings and are excellent as a condiment for dim sum, soups, stews, and noodle dishes. Because of its mild, subtly sweet taste, white rice vinegar is superb for flavoring with delicate herbs and flowers.

SHERRY VINEGAR

Rich, smooth, and mellow, sherry vinegar has a slightly nutty flavor with a sweet aftertaste. It is made near Jerez in southwestern Spain from the *oloroso* type of sherry that is produced without the *flor* yeast. Aged in wooden casks in the full heat of the sun, the vinegar develops a full-bodied flavor. The best sherry vinegars are made in a system much like that used to make balsamic vinegar, with some young vinegar added to oak casks containing older vinegar through a series of progressively smaller barrels over a period of two or three decades. Acidity is usually 6 to 7 percent.

Sherry vinegar blends well with olive, walnut, and hazelnut oils for marinades and salad dressings, and can be used extensively in cooking, especially with slightly sweet poultry dishes and with tomato-based soups and sauces. Use it to deglaze a pan after sautéing and with smoked poultry. It can be flavored with the medium to stronger herbs and seasonings.

PLUM VINEGAR, OR UME-SU

This Japanese delicacy is not a true vinegar at all, but rather the liquid that is drawn off the sour, immature umeboshi plums as they pickle in salt and shiso leaves *(Perilla frutescens).* In another misnomer, the plums are actually apricots, *Prunus mume.* A lovely, early-blooming tree hardy to 0°F, the mume plum is a favorite bonsai subject and ornamental tree in Japan. Native to China, it has been grown in Japan for 1,300 years.

Very salty, with a sweet and puckery citrus flavor, cherry fragrance, and lovely pink color, plum vinegar is added to salad dressings and to sauces, stews, soups, and steamed vegetables just before serving. Herbalists recommend it for its medicinal properties, as it eliminates lactic acid, alkalizes the digestive system, relieves indigestion, and strengthens the blood.

Wine Vinegar

As should be obvious, wine vinegar is made from wine, red, white, or rosé. Some wine vinegars are also made from the second pressing of the grapes used to make wine. Wine vinegars are the best vinegars for flavoring at home, with the white used for the lighter herbs and seasonings and the red for the more robust flavors. Quality runs the gamut. In her book, *Tastings* (Crown, 1986), Jenifer Harvey Lang reports finding no less than twenty-eight acceptable red wine vinegars, including ones from France, Italy, Greece, and the United States, while only seven were unacceptable. Acidity ranged from 5 to 7 percent. The price of the acceptable ones ranged from cheap to expensive. The only way to be sure of the quality is to compare the wine vinegars that are available in your area and note the ones you like. The best ones are generally made by the slow, or Orléans, process, but this is seldom stated on the label.

When cooking, the rich depth of flavor of red wine vinegar is well matched with dark meats and marinades, and is also good in salad dressings where the color is not a problem. The lighter, more mellow flavor of white wine vinegar is excellent with fish and light meats, accompanying marinades, pickles where a clear vinegar is better suited, most salad dressings, and butter sauces.

Other Vinegars

Some of the other vinegars you may find include those made from mead, fruit wines, potatoes, cashew nuts, molasses, pineapple, or any fermented liquor.

Making Vinegar at Home

If you have ever left a bottle of wine open only to discover some time later that it has turned to vinegar, you may think that making homemade vinegar is easy. If you are among the many others who, thanks to the vagaries of airborne bacteria, have ended up with only a malodorous, vile-tasting liquid, vinegar-making may seem to be a much more uncertain process. Another complication is that it is very difficult to measure the acidity of homemade vinegar, which is usually much lower than commercial vinegars. This is not a problem for general cooking purposes, but when it is used for preserving, vinegar must be at least 5 percent acidity for safety. Homemade vinegar should not be used for canning.

For those adventurous spirits who are willing to take the risks and necessary precautions, homemade vinegar promises the rewarding sense of self-satisfaction that comes from creating something personal and unique. To make vinegar, little more is needed than some form of ethyl alcohol, or ethanol, that is less than 18 percent alcohol; vinegar bacteria; a temperature of 59° to 86° F; and a nonreactive container.

Most often homemade vinegar is produced from red or white wine or alcoholic apple cider. When using wine, choose one that has good flavor and complexity, and is neither too cheap nor too expensive. Most commercial wines and ciders have sulfite preservatives, although a few preservative-free wines are now available. Preservatives will kill the vinegar bacteria. To get rid of the them, either shake the wine for five minutes in a large jar with lots of air space; pour the wine back and forth from one bottle to another for five minutes; or add ½ teaspoon of hydrogen peroxide to a fifth of wine and shake.

Cleanliness is very important, so make sure that all of your equipment and utensils are thoroughly washed and rinsed. Your hands and clothes should be clean as well. Use only glass, ceramic, plastic, or wooden containers, funnels, and so forth. Any glass bottle as well as pottery, porcelain, plastic, or enamel-coated metal can be used. *Never use reactive metals such as aluminum.* Choose a container size that allows for proportions of two to one, such as a gallon container for a yield of a half gallon of vinegar. Special wooden casks are available in 1-, 2-, 3-, 5-, and 10-gallon sizes from winemaking supply stores and mail-order suppliers. Fill wooden casks with water for two to three days to allow the wood to swell and seal. Casks should have a small spigot on one end near the top and a 2- to 3-inch bung hole in the top. Oak chips from a winemaking supply store can be added to nonwooden containers to get the wood flavor.

Although vinegar bacteria can naturally occur in the air, the surest way of introducing them into the alcohol is with a "mother." You may find mother of vinegar in local winemaking shops, or you can order it from one of the mail-order sources listed at the back of this book. Unpasteurized commercial vinegars usually will have the jellylike material in the bottle, and this can be used as well. A simple way of inoculating the alcohol with vinegar bacteria is to add a quart of unpasteurized wine or cider vinegar to each gallon of wine or cider. Put the alcohol in the container with the vinegar mother and cover the opening with cheesecloth or screen to keep out vinegar flies. Place it in a dark cupboard or closet that is room temperature. After two weeks to a month, smell and taste the liquid. If the vinegar develops a smell resembling acetone, it can be salvaged by pouring it back and forth between two containers several times. All of the alcohol should be converted to vinegar in anywhere from two to eight months.

When the vinegar is ready, you can draw off a bottle at a time, adding more wine and keeping the container no more than two-thirds full, or pour it all into well-cleaned smaller bottles and flavor it if desired. When bottling it, fill the bottle to the top, cap it tightly with a new cork or plastic cap, and store it in a cool, dark place. Some people prefer to kill the vinegar bacteria before bottling by heating the vinegar to 150° F or processing in a boiling-water bath for 5 minutes. For a mellower flavor, let the vinegar age for several months in the bottle before using.

FLAVORING VINEGAR

The handful of flavored vinegars available in stores pales by comparison with the infinite number of homemade varieties possible. In addition, homemade flavored vinegars have a fresher, more intense flavor and are very easy to make. What's so special about flavored vinegars? Simply put, they make anything that can be

Bottle your flavored vinegars in clean, attractive jars— recycled or fancy imports.

prepared with vinegar taste better without adding fat, salt, or a significant number of calories.

Besides herbs, you can use spices, fruits, flowers, and vegetables, alone or in combination, to flavor vinegars. Whatever you choose, there are a few simple basics to keep in mind.

As with making vinegar, cleanliness is essential. Wash all utensils, bottles, and containers with hot, soapy water, then rinse in hot water. The equipment needed includes containers for the steeping process. These can be any nonreactive material, such as glass, plastic, porcelain, pottery, or enamel-coated steel. They should have tight-fitting, nonreactive lids. If using canning jars or other containers with metal lids, place a piece of plastic wrap over the opening before putting on the lid. Other useful equipment includes a plastic or wooden spoon; plastic funnel; cheesecloth, muslin, coffee filters and holder, or nylon jelly bag; plastic strainer or colander; and glass or plastic measuring cups and spoons.

There are no hard-and-fast rules to making flavored vinegars, and instructions vary widely. The guidelines given in this book are the result of personal testing and taste. Experiment and vary the proportions to suit yourself. Keep a notebook with the proportions and combinations used so that you can accurately compare and repeat your favorites.

Most important is to use a vinegar that is the best you can afford and that you like even without flavoring. A bad vinegar will not improve with flavoring. Traditionally, flavored vinegars are most often made with red or white wine, rice, or cider vinegars, but experiment with others, especially sherry and the less-expensive balsamic vinegars. Freshly picked, homegrown herbs yield the best results, but purchased herbs are fine for those without gardening space. If necessary, even dried herbs are acceptable substitutes.

The length of time that the flavorings steep in the vinegar is also a matter of taste. Sample the vinegar after a week or so. Usually the greatest amount of flavor is extracted after a month. For extra-intense flavor, after a month strain the vinegar, add fresh flavoring, and continue steeping.

Although vinegars look beautiful in sunlight, the flavors are best maintained by steeping in a dark place at room temperature. Shake or stir contents occasionally,

making sure that the flavorings are always completely covered by vinegar so that they do not mold.

Once the flavor is to your liking, strain the vinegar. Either line a strainer or colander with a triple layer of cheesecloth, a single layer of muslin, or a nylon jelly bag, or use a coffee filter in a drip holder. If one straining does not yield a perfectly clear liquid, repeat the process. Strain into a container large enough to hold all of the vinegar.

After straining, use a funnel to pour the vinegar into clean glass bottles. Fill the bottles to the top and add a sprig of herb or a sampling of whatever was used to flavor the vinegar. There are many sources for bottles. Packrats will have saved empty salad dressing bottles, individual-serving wine bottles, ceramic-topped beer bottles, condiment bottles, and so forth. Import stores often carry interesting glass bottles. Local kitchen-supply and housewares stores and mail-order sources offer bottles specifically for vinegars. Whatever you choose, the lids should not be metal, but rather cork, plastic, ceramic, or glass. Use new corks, available from wine-supply or hardware stores.

Invest in a good bottle brush so that bottles can be scrupulously clean. To sterilize, wash bottles in hot soapy water, rinse in clean hot water, pour in some boiling water through a funnel, let stand for 10 minutes, and then drain. Let bottles rest upside down on clean towels. Alternatively, wash and rinse bottles well, then place them upright in a pan with 1 inch of water in the bottom. Place the pan in a preheated 350° F oven for 10 to 15 minutes.

Strain flavored vinegars through a coffee filter.

If you are capping your bottles with corks, seal them with wax and ribbon. Melt paraffin or sealing wax in an empty tin or orange juice can placed in a pan of water over low heat. Cut a 4-inch length of ribbon and place it over the corked bottle. Holding the ribbon firmly, dip the corked top of the bottle an inch or two into the melted wax. Let it cool, then repeat the process until the wax is thick.

When the bottles are filled and capped, apply labels. These can be as simple or elaborate as you want. Office supply stores have a selection of plain self-adhesive labels in different sizes. They also sell gold seals used by notaries. Herb, kitchen–supply, and housewares stores, as well as some bookstores, offer a range of decorative labels. Vinegar-makers with an artistic bent will want to create their own labels. This would be a good time to take that calligraphy class you've always been interested in. Felt-tip pens offer a range of colors, including gold and silver. An alternative is to make labels from heavy parchment paper or plain white or colored index cards. Punch a hole in the corner and tie it to the bottle with ribbon, yarn, or twine. (For labels to copy and use, see page 160.)

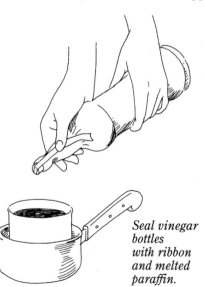

Seal vinegar bottles with ribbon and melted paraffin.

When giving a bottle of vinegar as a gift, consider writing a recipe for its use on a small card and tying it around the neck of the bottle. A gift basket might include several bottles of vinegar or some of the condiments or foods preserved with vinegar from the recipe section of this book. Whether you are giving them as gifts or keeping them for yourself, consider decorating special bottles of vinegar with a small dried herb bouquet or wreath.

Although vinegars look beautiful sitting on windowsills, the light and warmth dissipate the flavors. For their decorative effect, you might want to leave a few out, but for cooking, store the vinegar in a cool, dark place. Unopened, most vinegars will last a year or two, if not longer. Fruit vinegars do not keep quite as long as others.

Date bottles when you open them. Fruit vinegars tend to caramelize after opening and are best used within three months. Use others within three to six months of opening. When vinegar is more than six months old, taste it before using it to make sure the flavor is still good. Adding some fresh vinegar from time to time can preserve the flavor. Always keep vinegar bottles tightly capped. If a vinegar has mold floating on its surface, throw it away.

A delightful adjunct to making vinegar is collecting vinegar cruets. Whether fine antique cut crystal or Fifties kitsch, vinegar cruets from your collection are an interesting way to keep vinegar readily available on the kitchen counter or table. It's advisable to choose cruets with snug-fitting tops. Offering your favorite flavored vinegar and extra-virgin olive oil from an interesting pair of cruets can make your salads, steamed vegetables, and fresh bread all seem even more special.

HERBAL VINEGARS

Making your own herbal vinegars may not change your life, but it can certainly transform your culinary habits, as they can be used in virtually every aspect of cooking. They are the mainstay of flavored vinegars and are incredibly easy and inexpensive to make. With different vinegars and combinations of herbs as well as other ingredients, especially spices and fruits, the possible variations are practically limitless. Using a delicate rice wine vinegar with a subtle herb like chervil gives a dish a gentle hint of summer's glory. Combining a robust red wine vinegar with garlic, rosemary, and marjoram will add extra gusto to a hearty bean soup.

Vinegar served in cruets can make the simplest meal special.

Use about 1 cup of herb leaves to 2 cups of vinegar.

Herbs to consider for flavoring vinegars include all of the basils (anise, cinnamon, Genovese, Greek, lemon, lettuce leaf, Neapolitan, purple, ruffled green, and the tiny-leafed form), bay, borage, burnet, chervil, chives, dill, fennel (regular and bronze), garlic, garlic chives, lavender, lemon balm, lemongrass, lemon verbena, lovage, marjoram, oregano, parsley, rose geranium, rosemary, sage, savory, shallot, spearmint, sweet cicely, tarragon, and the thymes (especially French, English, and lemon).

The biggest mistake most people make when creating herbal vinegars is not using enough herbs. Several sprigs may give a whiff of the herb, but to really get an effect, use about 1 cup of loosely packed fresh herb leaves to 2 cups of vinegar. For dried herbs, use ½ cup for 2 cups of vinegar.

Gather fresh herbs by mid-morning after the dew has dried. Check for and remove insects. If the plants are muddy, gently wash and dry them with towels. Carefully strip the leaves from the stems. Place the herbs in a clean, sterilized jar and use a spoon to bruise them slightly. Pour the vinegar over the herbs and cover the jar tightly. Do not heat the vinegar. Let the herb-vinegar mixture steep in a dark place at room temperature. Shake the jar every couple of days and taste the vinegar after a week. If the flavor is not strong enough, let it stand for another one to three weeks, checking the flavor weekly. If an even stronger flavor is desired, repeat the steeping process with fresh herbs. When the flavor is right, strain the vinegar, fill the clean, sterilized bottles, cap them tightly, and label them.

Note that commercial mint vinegars are often sweetened with sugar and brightened with garish green food coloring. This is not to my taste, but if you prefer a sweetened mint vinegar, you can add sugar to taste to any of the mint vinegar recipes found here.

HERB VINEGAR COMBINATIONS

Apple Cider Vinegar	Dill, bay, and garlic
	Horseradish, shallot, and hot red pepper
	Dill, mustard seeds, lemon balm, and garlic
	Tarragon, chives, lemon balm, shallots, and garlic
	Garlic, basil, whole cracked nutmeg, and whole cloves
Champagne Vinegar	Lemon balm, lemon verbena, lemon thyme, lemongrass, and lemon zest
Malt Vinegar	Tarragon, garlic chives, whole cloves, and garlic or shallot

Red Wine Vinegar	Thyme, rosemary, hyssop, fennel, oregano, and garlic
	Basil, rosemary, tarragon, marjoram, mint, bay, dill seed, black peppercorns, and whole allspice berries and cloves
	Lemon thyme, rosemary, and black peppercorns
	Rosemary, savory, sage, basil, bay, and garlic
	Cilantro, sage, rosemary, bay, and hot red pepper
	Garlic, jalapeño peppers, and black peppercorns
	Basil, oregano, garlic, and black peppercorns
	Mint, rosemary, bay, sage, tarragon, garlic, and whole cloves, cinnamon stick, black peppercorns, allspice berries, and mustard seed
	Basil, mint, tarragon, rosemary, sage, garlic, fresh ginger root, bay, green onions, and whole allspice berries, cloves, mustard seeds, cumin seeds, black peppercorns, and cinnamon stick
	Thyme, rosemary, oregano, and basil
	Marjoram, basil, mint, dill, rosemary, bay, and whole allspice berries, black peppecorns, and cloves
	Sage, parsley, and shallots
	Burnet, borage, and dill
	Cilantro, hot red pepper, and garlic
	Lemongrass, lemon verbena, lemon zest, and green peppercorns
	Cilantro, garlic, and fresh ginger root
	Marjoram, burnet, and lemon balm
Sherry Vinegar	Basil, rosemary, tarragon, dill, sorrel, mint, chives, and garlic
	Parsley, thyme, rosemary, and bay
	Rosemary, oregano, sage, basil, parsley, garlic, and black peppercorns
	Shallot, thyme, and bay

Sherry Vinegar (cont'd)	Sage, whole allspice berries, cloves, and cinnamon stick
White Wine Vinegar	Basil, parsley, fennel, and garlic
	Tarragon, elder flowers, spearmint, lemon balm, shallot, garlic, and whole cloves and peppercorns
	Dill, basil, tarragon, and lemon balm
	Thai basil and hot red pepper
	Oregano, cilantro, garlic, and hot red pepper
	Mint, lemon balm, and lemon basil
	Rosemary, thyme, marjoram, savory, lavender, bay, garlic, and hot red pepper
	Orange mint, coriander seeds, garlic, and orange zest
	Marjoram, burnet, thyme, tarragon, parsley, and chives
	Tarragon, anise hyssop, hyssop, and lemon balm
	Basil, chives, garlic chives, tarragon, borage, and burnet
	Parsley, lovage, chervil, savory, thyme, rosemary, tarragon, shallots, and black peppercorns
	Tarragon, lemon thyme, and chive blossoms
	Mint and cardamom seeds
	Orange mint and orange zest
	Dill, mint, and garlic cloves
	Borage, dill, and shallots
	Tarragon, chervil, borage, watercress, garlic, and hot red pepper
	Savory, tarragon, chervil, basil, and chives

Spice Vinegars

Spice vinegars have a rich intensity and can be used in many ways, but they are especially satisfying with pickles, relishes, ketchups, chutneys, and marinades. Many different spices can be used, either alone or in combination with other spices or flavorings. The spices to try include allspice; cinnamon; cardamom; ginger; juniper; white, pink, black, and green peppercorns; Szechuan peppers; any of the chili peppers; nutmeg; and herb seeds, such as anise, dill, caraway, celery, coriander, cumin, and mustard. Use the spices in their whole form, not ground, and crush them just before adding the vinegar.

Although heating the vinegar is not usually recommended for flavored vinegars, it is beneficial with spiced vinegars because spices tend to be woody, and heating helps release the essential oils. Tie the spices in a square of muslin or cheesecloth for easy removal or put them into the vinegar loose and strain them out later. With either method, combine the spices and vinegar in a stainless steel saucepan and heat to 110° F. Immediately remove the pan from the heat and let the vinegar cool slightly before pouring it into the steeping container. Cover it tightly and set the container in a dark place at room temperature. Shake the container every couple of days and taste the vinegar after a week. Check the flavor weekly for up to a month until the desired flavor is reached. Remove or strain out the spices, then fill the bottles, cap them tightly, seal them, and add labels.

You can vary the proportions to your taste, but a reasonable amount is 2 to 4 tablespoons of seeds or spices to 2 cups of vinegar.

Spice Vinegar Combinations (for 2 cups vinegar)

Apple Cider Vinegar	1 teaspoon each whole cloves, black peppercorns, caraway seeds, 6 peeled whole garlic cloves
	2 teaspoons each allspice berries and coriander seeds, 1 teaspoon each mustard seeds and whole cloves, a 3-inch cinnamon stick, 1 bay leaf, and a 1-inch piece of fresh ginger root; or, substitute celery seeds for the coriander
Balsamic Vinegar	1 teaspoon each black peppercorns and whole cloves, 1 small hot red pepper, and a 1-inch piece of fresh ginger root
Malt Vinegar	2 teaspoons each allspice berries and coriander seeds, 1 teaspoon each mustard seeds and whole cloves, a 3-inch cinnamon stick, 1 bay leaf, and a 1-inch piece of fresh ginger root; or, substitute celery seeds for the coriander

Red Wine Vinegar	1 teaspoon each black, white, green, pink, and Szechuan peppercorns
	1 teaspoon each whole cloves, allspice berries, black peppercorns, cardamom seeds, and juniper berries, a 3-inch cinnamon stick, and 1 whole cracked nutmeg
Sherry Vinegar	1 teaspoon each black peppercorns and whole cloves, 1 small hot red pepper, and a 1" piece of fresh ginger root
	2 teaspoons each allspice berries and coriander seeds, 1 teaspoon each mustard seeds and whole cloves,a 3-inch cinnamon stick, 1 bay leaf, and a 1-inch piece of fresh ginger root; or, substitute celery seeds for the coriander
White Wine Vinegar	1 teaspoon each whole cloves, black peppercorns, caraway seeds, and 6 peeled whole garlic cloves

Fruit Vinegars

Fruit vinegars, including the ubiquitous raspberry vinegar that is so popular today, are nothing new. Many of the earliest vinegars were made from fruits such as dates and figs simply because they were abundant. In those days, the fermented liquid itself was made from the fruits. Today we usually flavor a wine or other vinegar with the fruit.

No matter how fruit vinegars are made or from what, they have a long heritage of providing pleasure to the palate or soothing comfort to the body. Warmed fruit vinegar taken with a spoonful of honey was a favored early remedy for sore throat. Today, fruit vinegars are popular for combining with sparkling water or a mixture of water and honey or sugar syrup and serving over ice, perhaps with a twist of lemon or orange peel. Of course, they can also be used in pies, sorbets, poached fruits, candies, and other sweets that call for vinegar as an ingredient, or they can be simply drizzled over fruit salads. Try fruit vinegars in a dressing for slaw, with fresh spinach, endive, radicchio, pak choi, or other greens, or as a marinade or baste for grilled or roasted meats or fruit. For instance, braise duck with cherry or orange vinegar, pork with plum or apricot, or fish with lemon or mango.

Raspberry is the most commonly used fruit in commercial vinegars. You may also occasionally spot cranberry, blueberry, or black currant vinegars in stores. But, just about any fruit can and has been used to make vinegar, including apricots, blackberries, blueberries, boysenberries, cherries, cranberries, currants (black, red, and white), dates, figs, gooseberries, huckleberries, kiwis, lemons, limes, loganberries, mangoes, marionberries, mulberries, nectarines, oranges, papayas, peaches, pears, persimmons, pineapples, plums, raisins, raspberries (red and yellow), rhubarb, strawberries, tangerines, and watermelons. Fruit vinegars can be made from dried fruit and frozen unsweetened fruit as well as from fresh fruit.

After you've decided what fruit to use, you'll have to decide how sweet a vinegar you want, as fruit vinegars often have some sugar or honey added. The most highly sweetened versions are usually used in drinks, and the more tart versions are reserved for cooking and salad dressings.

Over the years, I have found wide variation in proportions and techniques for making fruit vinegars. Obviously, there are many paths to the same destination. My preference is to make the process as easy as possible. Here are several tips to ensure success: First, use a vinegar that is at least 5 percent acidity. White and red wine vinegars are most often used, but experiment with others, matching flavors and intensities. Second, make sure the fruit is clean and dry, and if necessary, pitted. Peeling is optional.

Here's the simplest way to make fruit vinegars: Put the fruit, either cut up or mashed lightly, into a steeping container. Then, pour in enough vinegar to completely cover the fruit. Put the lid on tightly and store in a cool, dark place. Stir or shake every couple of days. Check the flavor after a week. If you want stronger flavor, continue steeping for up to three or four weeks, tasting weekly. For an even more intense flavor, you can strain and repeat the steeping process with fresh fruit. When the flavor is just right, strain the mixture and pour it into a stainless-steel or enameled-steel pan. Add sugar or honey, in the proportions of ¼ to 1 cup of sugar or 3 tablespoons to ¾ cup of honey to each 4 cups of vinegar. (Some people use more, but these are my personal limits.) Bring the mixture to a simmer, stirring frequently, and cook for 3 minutes. Don't let it boil. Skim off any foam that develops, let the vinegar cool, and pour it into sterilized bottles through a funnel. Add a few pieces of fruit if desired, cap the bottles tightly, seal them, and add labels.

Citrus vinegars are easy and quick. Simply cut the fruit into quarters or sixths, place the pieces in a bottle, pour in vinegar, and cap the bottle tightly. The vinegar will be ready to use after a week or so. Use citrus vinegars within six months. Some people prefer using the zest, juice, and pulp of citrus fruits, discarding the bitter white inner peel.

Fruit Vinegar Combinations

Champagne Vinegar	Peaches and cinnamon basil
	Pears and hyssop
Red Wine Vinegar	Raspberries and thyme
	Sweet cherries, anise seed, and tarragon
	Tangerines, a cinnamon stick, allspice berries, and whole cloves

Red Wine Vinegar *(cont'd)*	Cranberries, orange mint, orange zest, and a cinnamon stick
	Cranberries, orange mint, orange zest, and a cinnamon stick
Rice Wine Vinegar	Nectarines and allspice berries
	Mangoes, papayas, garlic chives, fresh ginger root, and lemongrass
Rose Wine Vinegar	Raspberries, rose geranium, and rose petals
Sherry Vinegar	Peaches and anise hyssop
	Apricots and allspice berries
White Wine Vinegar	Raspberries and bee balm flowers and leaves
	Raspberries, rose geranium, and rose petals
	Strawberries, a cinnamon stick, and a cracked nutmeg
	Strawberries and spearmint
	Nectarines and allspice berries
	Blueberries, lemon thyme, and a cinnamon stick
	Blueberries and orange mint
	Blueberries and purple basil
	Any bramble berry or blueberries and lavender flowers
	Blackberries, lemon balm, and a cinnamon stick
	Lemons, oranges, and limes with lemon balm, lemon thyme, and orange mint
	Tangerines, a cinnamon stick, allspice berries, and whole cloves
	Cranberries and rosemary
	Rhubarb, angelica or sweet cicely, and candied ginger
	Gooseberries, currants, and garlic chives leaves and flowers

Floral Vinegars

More than any other flavored vinegar, those made with flowers call up gentle images. Imagine an Edwardian afternoon tea with blueberries and strawberries macerated in lavender vinegar, or perhaps crystal bottles of shimmering pastel liquids during a soothing, leisurely bath fragrant with rose petal vinegar; luncheon on a sunny terrace featuring a succulent salad of fresh, crisp mixed greens garnished with peppery nasturtium blossoms matched to a nasturtium vinaigrette.

Choose from among edible flowers like those of anise hyssop, basil, borage, calendula, carnations and pinks, chamomile, chives, dill, elder, fennel, garlic chives, lavender, lovage, marjoram, mint, nasturtium, oregano, primrose, rose, rose-scented geranium, thyme, and violets. **Never use poisonous flowers or those that may have been treated with hazardous chemicals, such as flowers from a florist.** You can use any vinegars because florial flavors tend to be somewhat subtle, champagne, white or rosé wine vinegar, or rice vinegar is often best. However, with certain combinations, other vinegars are also possible.

The flowers should be freshly picked, clean, and dry; use only the petals, removing the green sepals and stem. Place the petals in a steeping container and cover them with the vinegar. One cup of loosely packed flowers to 2 cups of vinegar, but feel free to consider using even more of the flowers. Cover the container tightly, store it in a dark place at room temperature. Check the flavor after one week. Continue steeping for several more weeks if a stronger flavor is desired. Strain, fill bottles, add a few fresh flowers, cap tightly, seal, label, and store.

Floral Vinegar Combinations

Apple Cider Vinegar	Nasturtium flowers and leaves, shallot, garlic, and hot red pepper
	Nasturtium, garlic chive, and dill flowers
Champagne Vinegar	Rose flowers and lemon balm leaves
Red Wine Vinegar	Lovage, oregano, marjoram, and basil flowers
	Rose and violet flowers
	Nasturtium flowers and leaves, shallot, garlic, and hot red pepper
Rice Vinegar	Chive and garlic chive flowers
	Calendula, lemon thyme, and lemon basil flowers, and lemon zest
	Anise hyssop, fennel, and Mexican marigold mint flowers
Sherry Vinegar	Elder flowers and candied ginger

White Wine Vinegar	Chive and garlic chive flowers
	Chive flowers and summer savory leaves
	Borage and burnet flowers
	Carnation or cottage pink flowers, a cinnamon stick, and whole cloves
	Lavender and mint flowers
	Chive, fennel, dill, lavender, borage, and mint flowers

VEGETABLE VINEGARS

Vegetable vinegars are the least known of the flavored vinegars. They offer intensified vegetable flavors in a liquid form. The vegetables most often used are cucumbers; all types of onions and their relatives, including shallots, garlic, green onions, sweet onions, and red, yellow, or white onions; and both hot and sweet peppers. Use a single vegetable or combine several, with herbs and spices as optional additions. Quantities are variable, but a good proportion is 1 to 2 cups of chopped vegetables to 4 cups of vinegar. Slice, peel, remove the seeds, or otherwise prepare the vegetables, place them in a nonreactive container, add herbs or spices if desired, and pour in the vinegar. Make sure enough vinegar is added to totally cover the vegetables. Cover tightly. Let the vinegar steep for a week, then taste it. Continue steeping until the desired flavor is reached, for up to three more weeks. Strain and bottle, cap tightly, and add labels.

VEGETABLE VINEGAR COMBINATIONS

Apple Cider Vinegar	Cucumber, shallot, garlic chives, and black peppercorns
	Green onions, sweet and hot peppers, sweet onions, shallots, and garlic cloves
Red Wine Vinegar	Sweet red pepper, hot red peppers, garlic, rosemary, and tarragon
White Wine Vinegar	Cucumber and dill seed and leaves
	Sweet peppers, whole allspice and cloves, a cinnamon stick, and fresh ginger root
	Green onions, green peppercorns, thyme, marjoram, and a bay leaf
	Onion, fennel, and tarragon

CHAPTER 3

GROWING YOUR OWN HERBS

Because gardening is my passion as well as my profession, all types of plants fascinate me. None, however, weave their magic as do herbs. Even the smallest planting of herbs offers the rewards suggested by the saying, "When all else fails, there is always the garden." What is it that makes herbs so appealing? Is it their scent? The fact that the plants have changed little through the ages? Their plethora of flavors? Their healing properties? For each of us the siren's song may have a slightly different tune, but few can deny the sustenance and solace that herbs offer. When walking among my herbs, I am linked to generations of gardeners before me who have experienced the same pleasures.

I've grown herbs in places and with methods as diverse as in a suburban yard in the cool and rainy Pacific Northwest, in the cramped shady space behind a Manhattan brownstone, in raised beds on a Midwestern farm, and in containers on an urban terrace in the Upper South. From these varied experiences, I can state with confidence that herbs freely adapt to a variety of climates and soils, have a minimum of pests, and generally are easy to grow.

CREATING AN HERB GARDEN

Herbs are versatile both in the garden and in the kitchen. They are readily incorporated into the landscape, either alone or with flowers, bulbs, trees, shrubs, fruits, and vegetables. Some pragmatic gardeners simply plant the herbs in rows along with the vegetables. This method works particularly well with herbs that you want in large quantities, such as dill and basil. Most gardeners, however, prefer to plant their herbs either among flowers or in a special area devoted solely to herbs.

When assimilating herbs with flowers, they can be treated as you would any annual or perennial. Choose and place the plants according to their color, texture, size, form, and bloom. For a garden specifically devoted to herbs, there are many possibilities for design. One popular design is the traditional four-square garden centered with a sundial or other garden ornament. Herb beds can also border a walk or line a fence or wall. Whatever your design, the cultivated area should be no wider than 4 or 5 feet so that you can easily tend the plants without walking frequently on the soil and compacting it. Place taller plants toward the back or, if the bed is to be viewed from all sides, in the center. Place progressively shorter plants toward the front or outer edges.

Growing Conditons for Herbs

Many of our favorite culinary herbs are from the Mediterranean region, so it's not surprising that they like full sun and are tolerant of poor, dry soil. Full sun means at least six hours of direct sun each day. If that is not available in your yard, don't despair.

Certain herbs tolerate light shade, or about four hours a day of direct sun. These include angelica, bee balm, burnet, chamomile, chervil, coriander, dill, fennel, hyssop, lemon balm, lovage, mint, parsley, rosemary, sweet cicely, tarragon, thyme, and violet.

When large areas that receive at least four hours of sun are not available, look around your yard for even the smallest space that gets sufficient light. For instance, what about the front steps, the area around a lamp post, or just outside the kitchen door? Several large pots or a whiskey barrel cut in half do not take up much room and can hold enough herbs to flavor a lovely array of vinegars.

Some gardeners contend that the soil for herbs shouldn't be enriched at all — that their flavor is not as good when plants are grown in fertile earth. I am of the philosophy that all living things benefit from at least a little tender loving care, so no matter what the condition of my soil I work in some compost or well-rotted manure. Organic matter such as this benefits both clay soil, by opening it up, and sandy soil, by helping retain water. Of utmost importance is that the soil be well-drained. Surviving winter is especially difficult for perennial and shrubby herbs in poorly drained soil. One particularly good means for making sure that drainage is adequate is to plant your herbs in raised beds.

When planting herbs in an area that has never been cultivated before, remove all grass, weeds, or other growth, then till or dig the soil deeply — at least 8 to 10 inches deep, but preferably 12 to 18 inches. Ideally, do this in the fall, working in organic matter, so that the soil is ready for planting the following spring.

Whether the area has been previously gardened or not, make sure you're providing the right conditions by having your soil tested by a laboratory or by using a testing kit available at garden centers. Follow the recommendations from the lab or from the kit for soil amendments. The ideal pH range for herbs is 6.2 to 6.8, or slightly acidic. Use a complete organic fertilizer, such as 2-3-2 or 5-10-5. A good rule of thumb is about five pounds per hundred square feet. Organic matter such as compost and manure and organic commercial fertilizers release their nutrients slowly, so herbs are well fed without being oversatiated, as can happen with chemical fertilizers.

Herbs do well in most temperate climates that receive an average amount of rainfall. The gardener's rule of thumb of one inch of water a week applies to herbs.

If there's insufficient rain, water deeply once a week with a porous soaker hose, or water with a water-breaker on the end of a hose. The best time to water is in early morning. As an alternative, install a drip-watering system. To conserve moisture and keep down weeds, apply three to five inches of an organic mulch, such as compost, shredded leaves, straw, or buckwheat or cocoa hulls.

PLANTING

The fastest and easiest way to get an herb garden started is to buy young plants at a garden center or plant sale. These are ready for transplanting to the garden as soon as the soil is warm. The hardier perennial and annual herbs can be set out several weeks before the last frost, although there is some risk involved if an especially hard frost comes. It is important to wait until all danger of frost has passed before planting tender annuals.

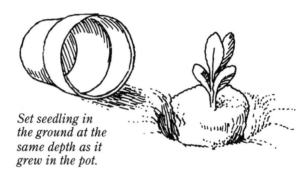

Set seedling in the ground at the same depth as it grew in the pot.

When you are ready to plant, choose a day that is cool. The best planting time is late afternoon on a day when rain is expected in the next twenty-four to thirty-six hours. Gently remove the plant from its pot. If the roots are matted on the outside of the soil ball, loosen them with your fingers. Use a hand trowel to dig a hole in the soil. Set the plant in the ground at the same depth as it sat in the pot, fill in around the roots with soil, and firm the soil gently. Water well.

Starting plants from seed, either indoors in early spring or directly in the garden in late spring, is pleasurable to some and an ordeal to others. For most herbs you'll need only one or two plants, so buying a whole package of seeds can be wasteful. For herbs you want to have in large quantities, starting your own plants from seed is a logical endeavor. Many of the perennial herbs are particularly slow and difficult to germinate, but the annuals are much easier. Some herbs, such as borage, dill, fennel, and parsley, do not transplant well, and these are best sown directly into the garden.

If you decide to start your own plants, plan on sowing the seeds indoors four to eight weeks before the estimated date for planting them outdoors. Use clay pots or seed flats filled with moistened sterile soil-less potting mix, which you can buy at any garden center. Make shallow rows or depressions in the potting mix, put in the seeds to the depth recommended on the packet, and cover with sand or potting mix. Mist with water to moisten, then cover with glass or plastic to maintain humidity. Place the pots or flats in an area with a constant temperature of 65° to 70°F, preferably with bottom heat. When the seeds have germinated, remove the cover and place the pots or flats in a sunny window or under fluorescent or high-pressure grow-lights. When it's necessary to thin seedlings, use a scissors rather than pulling them out, to avoid disturbing the roots of the remaining plants. You can transplant

Water seed tray gently to avoid
disturbing seeds. Cover with plastic.

Thin seedlings by clipping away extra
plants with scissors.

large seedlings to individual pots when they are several inches tall. Feed your seedlings with a water-soluble fertilizer, such as fish emulsion. Keep them well-watered at all stages.

Because there are so many different kinds of herbs with different growth habits, this very generic description of starting seeds will not apply to every plant. Consult a comprehensive herb book for greater detail on propagating herbs.

CONTAINERS, INDOORS AND OUT

Herbs take to containers like ducks to water. Growing them as houseplants is a bit more of a challenge than growing them outdoors in containers, but both methods make it possible to have fresh herbs readily available. Even herb growers with large yards find that gardening in containers has many advantages. For people with little or no gardening space, containers save the day. One benefit of containers is their portability. You can rearrange the "garden" according to need, desire, pleasure, and whim. Pots and railing boxes filled with lush greenery soften the lines and angles of a porch, deck, or terrace. Placing planters on pedestals adds the dimension of height to a grouping or showcases a single planting.

Place large pots of
herbs on dollies so
that you can move
them easily.

Containers are available in a wide array of materials. Clay and terra-cotta are classic choices, but they are also heavy, easily damaged by freezing and thawing, and tend to dry out more quickly than other materials. Concrete is heavy and needs special treatment to blend in with the landscape. Plastic and fiberglass are generally inexpensive, lightweight, and come in a wide range of sizes and styles. (Some gardeners avoid plastic because it is made from petrochemicals.) Wooden pots are available in styles ranging from rustic half whiskey barrels to specially constructed containers that match your home. If you use containers made with pressure-treated wood for herbs or any edible plants, you should line the containers with plastic sheeting before filling them. This prevents the chemicals used to treat the wood from leaching into the soil and being absorbed by the plants.

Whatever containers you choose, they must have drainage holes to keep the soil from becoming waterlogged. You can usually drill holes into pots that don't already have them. In selecting a container, match the size to the plant. Most individual herbs can be grown in something as small as a standard 6- or 8-inch round pot. If you are growing a mixture of herbs in one container, choose larger pots suited to the size and number of plants. To increase the mobility of large, heavy planters, attach casters or use a plant dolly.

Container plantings are most attractive when they are overflowing, so plan for no more than 8 to 12 inches between plants, depending on their anticipated size at maturity. Bear in mind that container-grown plants seldom grow as large as garden-grown plants. When designing container plantings, combine upright, bushy, and trailing plants for maximum effect. Include plants with edible flowers to brighten the green palette.

Garden soil is too dense to work well in containers. "Soil-less" potting mixes are lighter and offer better drainage. Commercial mixes use peat moss as the main ingredient. Since depleting peat bogs is becoming an environmental issue, consider making your own homemade equivalent from equal parts of compost, pulverized pine or fir bark, and perlite or vermiculite. For every cubic foot of mix you're making, add four ounces of dolomitic limestone, one pound of rock phosphate or colloidal phosphate, four ounces of greensand, one pound of granite dust, and two ounces of blood meal or three ounces of cottonseed or soybean meal.

Watering and feeding of container plantings during the growing season are crucially important because the plants have limited root space. Feed them every two weeks with an organic water-soluble fertilizer, such as fish emulsion, manure or compost tea, or seaweed extract. How frequently you water depends on many factors, including weather as well as plant and pot size. Check the plants daily, water them *thoroughly* every time you do water, and keep the soil evenly moist. Hardy perennial plants can be overwintered either by wrapping the pots with some type of insulating material, such as bubble wrap, or by moving them to a sheltered spot outdoors or into an unheated garage or cellar after they are dormant. You can also bring plants indoors while they are still actively growing and treat them as houseplants during the winter.

Growing herbs as houseplants requires a bright sunny location with cool temperatures. Provide daytime temperatures of 60° to 72° F and nighttime temperatures of 50° to 60° F. You'll have the most success with fluorescent and high-pressure grow-lights. Grouping plants together helps to increase the humidity, as does placing them on a pebble-filled tray.

HARVESTING

The highest concentration of flavor in herbs usually occurs just before they flower, so that's the best time to harvest them for drying. Try to do your harvesting in the early morning, after the dew has dried. For cooking and making vinegar, I gather herbs whenever it best suits my schedule and when the plants have enough foliage so that growth is not impeded. I pick flowers when they are at their peak. To gather seeds, cut the stalks before the seeds begin to scatter, and hang them upside down in a paper bag. The bag will catch the seeds as they fall.

Household Uses and Hints

lthough making and using flavored vinegars in cooking brings me pleasure, the many other household, health, and beauty uses of vinegar never cease to intrigue me. The fact that such a simple substance as vinegar can accomplish such a wide range of tasks reinforces my belief in the natural order of things. Laboratories may develop all manner of complex chemicals, yet for many of the same uses, vinegar, a substance that has been around for thousands of years, is a safer alternative.

Around the House

The mildly acid nature of vinegar makes it useful for a wide range of cleaning chores and other tasks around the home. Inexpensive, with no noxious fumes or additives, a gallon of distilled white or apple cider vinegar can replace a number of other bottles and boxes often found in the cupboard and closet.

Polish furniture. Wipe furniture with a soft clean cloth moistened with a mixture of 3 tablespoons vinegar and 1 quart water. This also removes cloudy film from varnished surfaces. Rub with grain of the wood. Polish with a soft dry cloth.

Furniture oil to deter woodworm. Make a furniture polish and woodworm deterrent in one by combining 5 ounces linseed oil, 5 ounces turpentine, 2 ounces vinegar, and 2 ounces denatured alcohol. Shake well; apply with a soft clean cloth.

Remove water rings on wooden furniture. Combine vinegar and olive oil in equal parts. On a clean soft cloth, work mixture with the grain to erase water rings.

Remove stains on wood. To remove dark stains from wood floors or furniture, first clean the area with coarse steel wool dipped in mineral spirits. Next, scrub the stain with vinegar, allowing it to penetrate for several minutes. Repeat, if necessary, then rinse with water and wax.

Brighten carpet. Rejuvenate carpet colors by brushing with a mixture of 1 cup vinegar in 1 gallon of water.

Leather furniture polish. Bring 2 cups of linseed oil to a boil and boil for 1 minute; cool. Stir in 1 cup vinegar. Shake well; apply with a clean soft cloth. Or, mix equal parts of linseed oil and vinegar, shake well, and apply with a clean soft cloth.

Remove carpet or rug stains. While the stain is still fresh, apply a mixture of 1 part vinegar to 3 parts water and let it stand for a few minutes. Sponge from the center out and blot with a dry cloth. Repeat, if necessary.

Remove chewing gum. Vinegar removes gum from fabric, carpet, and upholstery.

Remove stickers, decals, and glue. Apply vinegar directly or with a clean soft cloth to remove price tags, bumper stickers, decals, or glue.

Loosen old glue on furniture joints. When disassembling furniture rungs and joints to reglue, fill a squirt bottle with vinegar and apply to the joint.

Remove mildew. Use vinegar at full strength or mixed with water to remove mildew from clothing, furniture, bathroom fixtures, shower curtains, and so forth.

Clean plastic upholstery. Wipe plastic or vinyl upholstery with a soft cloth dampened with a solution of water and vinegar.

Make plastic anti-static. Vinegar decreases static and attraction of dust on plastic and vinyl. Wipe upholstery with a cloth dampened with a vinegar-water solution. Add a pour of vinegar to rinse water when laundering plastic curtains or tablecloths.

Clean up pet or people "accidents." Sprinkle vinegar on soiled area, wait a few minutes, then sponge from the center out. Blot with a dry cloth. Repeat, if necessary. Alternatively, combine a small amount of liquid detergent and 3 tablespoons vinegar in 1 quart of warm water. Sponge on soiled area until clean, rinse with a cloth dampened with warm water, then blot with a dry cloth.

Remove perspiration odors. Wipe or rinse article with vinegar.

Remove cooking odors. Prevent the odor of boiling cabbage by adding a little vinegar to the cooking water. To remove the odor of fish or onions from your hands, wipe them with vinegar. Pour vinegar into the hot skillet or pan after cooking fish or onions and let it simmer for a few minutes. Boil 1 tablespoon of vinegar in 1 cup of water to eliminate cooking odors from the room.

Remove room odors. Place bowls of vinegar in a room to remove the odors of smoke, paint, vomit, or other substances.

Clean brass, bronze, and copper. Mix vinegar with baking soda or salt to make a paste. Once the tarnish is removed, rinse with clear water. To keep copper pans shiny, wipe with a solution of vinegar and salt after each use.

Polish chrome and stainless steel. Moisten a soft cloth with vinegar and polish.

Clean aluminum utensils. Remove dark stains from the inside of aluminum utensils by adding vinegar to boiling water and simmering until clean.

Scour pots and pans. Mix equal amounts of flour and salt. Make a paste with vinegar. Rub on pans with a sponge; rinse. Remove normal food stains by soaking pots and pans in full-strength vinegar for 30 minutes, then wash in hot soapy water and rinse.

Metal primer. Prime galvanized metal before painting by scouring it with vinegar.

Wash windows and mirrors. Several variations of window cleaner can be made at home. 1) Mix 1 tablespoon of vinegar in 1 quart of water. 2) Mix 1 to 2 tablespoons of vinegar and 3 to 8 tablespoons of ammonia in 1 quart of water. 3) Mix ¼ cup each of vinegar and ammonia with 1 tablespoon of cornstarch in 1 quart of water.

Clean walls, woodwork, and blinds. Mix 1 cup ammonia, ½ cup vinegar, and ¼ cup baking soda in 1 gallon warm water. Apply with sponge or soft cloth; rinse.

Wash dishes. To cut the grease on dishes, add a capful of vinegar to the dishwater.

Rinse crystal and glassware. Crystal and glassware will sparkle easily when rinsed in a solution of one part vinegar to three parts warm water.

Clean bottles, jars, and vases. Remove chalky mineral film on bottles, jars, and vases by pouring in vinegar, letting it stand for several minutes. If needed, let it stand for a longer period, then shake or brush vigorously. To use in a dishwasher, place a cup of vinegar on the bottom rack, run the machine for 3 to 5 minutes, replace the vinegar with a fresh cup, then complete the dishwashing cycle with dishwasher detergent.

Clean coffee and tea stains from glass and china. Boil vinegar in glass coffee pots once a week, wash, and rinse. Equal parts vinegar and salt removes stains from cups.

Freshen lunch boxes. To make lunch boxes fresh-smelling, dampen a piece of bread with vinegar and leave overnight in the closed box.

Remove lime deposits. Tea kettles, coffee brewers, and irons can accumulate lime deposits from hard water. To clean, fill with vinegar and heat or run through one cycle. Rinse well or run through another cycle with plain water before using.

Open clogged drains. Bring vinegar to a boil and pour a small amount down the drain. Let it sit for 5 to 10 minutes, then run hot water. Repeat, if necessary. Alternatively, pour a handful of baking soda in the drain, add ½ cup vinegar, cover drain and let sit for 5 to 10 minutes, then run cold water.

Clean oven. Apply vinegar at full strength with a sponge to the door and walls.

Sharpen knives. When sharpening knives, dampen the whetstone with vinegar.

Loosen rusted, corroded screws and hinges. Pour vinegar over the head of a rusty screw or a hinge to loosen it. Clean rusty screws, bolts, and nuts by soaking them in vinegar, scrubbing them with a brush, if necessary.

Clean corroded shower and faucet heads. Unscrew and remove clogged, corroded shower and faucet heads and screens, place in a small container and cover with vinegar. Let soak for several hours or overnight.

Improve light from propane lamps. For more light with less fuel from a propane lamp, remove mantle, place in container, and cover with vinegar. Let soak for several hours. Dry thoroughly before using.

Season new skillets. To keep foods from sticking in new skillets, first boil some vinegar in the pan.

Dye Easter eggs. For bright Easter egg colors, combine ½ cup boiling water, 1 teaspoon vinegar, and 1 teaspoon food coloring. Dip eggs until color as desired.

Remove dried paint on glass. Apply heated vinegar to paint on window glass to soften.

Keep hiking or camping water fresh. Add several drops of vinegar to a canteen or insulated container of water to keep it fresh longer and make it a better thirst-quencher.

Make windshields frost-free. Wipe windshields with a sponge soaked in a solution of three parts vinegar to one part water to prevent frost from forming on them.

Cut-flower solution. Keep cut flowers fresh longer by adding 2 tablespoons of vinegar and 1 tablespoon of sugar to each quart of warm (100° F) water.

Kill grass and weeds. Unwanted grass and weeds along the edge of driveways or between stepping stones meet their demise when you pour vinegar on them.

Deter fleas and ticks. Adding a teaspoon of vinegar to each quart of your pet's drinking water acts systematically to deter fleas and ticks.

Clean stiff, caked paint brushes. Soak mildly caked paint brushes in vinegar until clean and soft. For worse cases, bring vinegar to simmer, put in brushes, and continue heating gently for 5 to 10 minutes. Wash in warm, soapy water; rinse well.

Remove cement from hands. To clean up hands after working in cement or concrete, wash hands in vinegar, then rinse in water.

Remove fruit stains from hands. Rub hands with vinegar to remove fruit stains.

Make wrapping tape adhere better. Add a few drops of vinegar to the water used to moisten wrapping tape.

Check calcium supplements. To check the absorbability of calcium supplements, drop them into vinegar. If they dissolve quickly, then they are of good quality.

Repel ants. Ants will stay away from a kitchen or any area wiped down or sprayed with a solution of equal parts water and vinegar.

Repel cats in the garden. Soak pieces of paper in vinegar and put around the garden.

Animal acceptance. A Kentucky dairy farmer reports that a new cow is quickly accepted into the herd when she is sprayed with a solution of vinegar and water.

Seed starting. To improve germination of woody-coated seeds (asparagus, cardinal climber, cypress vine, lupine, moonflower vine, morning glory, okra, and sweet peas) rub seeds between two sheets of coarse sandpaper, then soak overnight in a pint of warm water with ½ cup of vinegar and a squirt of liquid soap. Use water treatment without sandpaper for nasturtium, parsley, parsnip, and beet seeds.

Vinegar painting. Decorate finished or unfinished wooden picture frames, furniture, or other objects with a texturizing tool and a vinegar-paint solution. To make the paint, mix ½ cup white vinegar, 1 teaspoon granulated sugar, and a squeeze of clear liquid dish detergent. In a second container, place 2 tablespoons of dry powdered poster paint and add enough vinegar solution to make a mixture that doesn't run when brushed on a vertical surface. Brush the solution on the surface, and then use a texturing tool, such as a comb, a feather, a crumpled paper, or a sponge, to create the desired effect. To try again, wipe clean with a rag and distilled vinegar. When done, let the paint dry thoroughly, then apply several coats of clear polyurethane.

Clean and restore lustre to patent leather. Wipe with soft clean cloth moistened with vinegar.

Clean salt marks on leather. Wipe salt-stained boots or shoes with a soft clean cloth moistened with vinegar.

Remove fabric creases and thread holes. When lengthening a hem, changing a crease, or opening a seam, make a solution of equal parts vinegar and water, then use it to dampen a pressing cloth, pressing as usual.

Make sharp creases. Dampen fabric with cloth moistened with solution of 1 part vinegar to 2 parts water. Place heavy brown paper over the crease and press.

Clean electric iron. To remove dark or burned spots on the bottom of an iron, rub with a mixture of vinegar and salt, heat in an aluminum pan, then rinse with clean water.

Remove scorch marks. With soft clean cloth dampened with vinegar, lightly rub scorched fabric. Wipe with clean cloth. Not effective on heavily scorched items.

Iron without shine. To keep wool and other fabrics from becoming shiny when ironing, place a cloth dampened with 1 part vinegar to 2 parts water over the fabric.

Launder shower curtains. To remove mildew and soap scum from plastic shower curtains, launder the curtain with a bath towel in the washing machine, adding a cup of vinegar during the rinse cycle.

Rinse silk. After hand-washing silk clothing in mild soap, remove soap residue by adding a capful of vinegar to clean, cool rinse water. Roll in towel to remove excess water; hang to dry until slightly damp. Press on wrong side with dry iron.

Prolong life of hose and lingerie. Add vinegar to the rinse water.

Laundry rinse water. Get rid of excess suds in either hand or machine washes by adding a cup of vinegar to the rinse water, followed by a clear-water rinse.

Make clothes whiter. Add 1½ cups vinegar to rinse water to brighten laundry.

Make fabric color-fast. Immerse fabrics in vinegar before washing.

Set fabric dye. After dyeing fabric, set the color by adding 1 cup of vinegar to the last rinse water.

Remove wine and ketchup stains from washable cotton polyester and blends. Sponge with vinegar within 24 hours. Launder as usual.

Remove non-oily stains. Remove non-oily, water-soluble stains such as wine, perspiration, fruit juice, alcoholic drinks, coffee, tea, soft drinks, salt water, or vomit from carpet, furniture, and fabric by one of several methods. For washable clothing, either dab the area with a clean soft cloth dampened in vinegar or soak the garment in a mixture of 3 parts vinegar to 1 part cool water. For upholstery and carpet, mix 1 to 2 teaspoons each of vinegar and liquid detergent in 2 cups of lukewarm water, then apply the mixture gently with a soft brush or towel. Rinse with clean water, repeating if necessary, then dry by blotting or with a fan or hair dryer.

Remove crayon stains. Moisten a soft toothbrush with vinegar and rub out crayon from fabric or other surfaces.

Remove deodorant stains. To remove stains from deodorants and antiperspirants, lightly rub fabric with vinegar, then launder as usual.

Remove ink stains. Remove ink marks from fabric by moistening the area with vinegar or by wiping it with a vinegar-dampened clean soft cloth.

Remove rust stains from fabric. Moisten washable fabric with vinegar, then rub in some salt. Place in sun to dry, then launder as usual.

Keep linens from yellowing. Vinegar in the rinse water of linens, such as tablecloths, napkins, sheets, and pillowcases, keeps them from yellowing in storage.

Soften blankets and sweaters. Add 2 cups of vinegar to rinse water to remove soap odor and make material soft and fluffy.

Home Remedies

Several thousand years before humans discovered the gustatory delight of pickles, they were using vinegars for medicinal and cosmetic properties. Both ancient Eastern and Western cultures depended on vinegar for its internal and external therapeutic values. This salubrious elixir was prescribed by Hippocrates as early as 400 B.C., and the ancient Greeks and Romans used it for such diverse purposes as an aid to digestion, a scurvy preventative, and a fat neutralizer. Vinegar's antiseptic and antibacterial qualities made it an important commodity during times of disease.

When Victorian ladies used vinegar as a skin tonic, hair rinse, and bath additive, they were carrying on a long tradition. In his classic book, *Folk Medicine*, D. C. Jarvis, M.D., elaborates on a number of home remedies, most of which are based on apple cider vinegar. Other people have also made a variety of claims for the beneficial effects of apple cider vinegar, including improving body metabolism, boosting the immune system, aiding in the prevention of osteoporosis, increasing hormone levels, lowering cholesterol, and acting as an antioxidant.

In her book *Colonial Kitchen Herbs and Remedies*, Ferne Shelton writes that a tonic of 2 teaspoons of vinegar in 1 cup of water as a beverage with meals was used in early America to alleviate a dull memory, overeating, eye, ear, and nose trouble, coughs and laryngitis, asthma, creaking joints, facial tics, food poisoning, digestive problems, thinning hair, sore mouth and gums, fragile fingernails, dandruff, skin rashes, and general fatigue.

In the remedies that follow, consider using wine or rice vinegars as well as apple cider vinegar.

NOTE: *Herbal vinegar made specifically for cosmetic and therapeutic purposes with nonculinary herbs should not be taken internally.*

Facial Tonics

Cosmetic vinegars — also called toilet vinegars — have been an indispensable complexion aid for centuries. Able to close pores and preserve or restore the skin's natural acidity, or proper pH balance, vinegars keep both oily and dry complexions soft and fresh. Vinegar tonics are much better for the skin than most commercial tonics because the latter usually contain drying alcohol. Vinegar tonics also combat the ravages of alkaline soaps and makeup. Depending on the herbs infused in the vinegar, tonics can tone, heal, soothe, or soften the skin of both women and men. They can also keep acne at bay, improve circulation, reduce broken veins and capillaries, smooth out wrinkles, and bleach freckles.

To use vinegar as a facial skin tonic, dilute it with six parts of spring water, rose water, or orange flower water and splash or spritz it on your face after washing, or apply the mixture with a cotton ball.

For cosmetic use, choose a high-quality apple cider vinegar or an herb-infused cider or wine vinegar, prepared as any culinary herb vinegar. Homemade herbal cosmetic vinegars can be as strong or as delicate as you like. A good proportion to start with is 1 cup of fresh petals or leaves for each 2 cups of vinegar, steeped for several weeks and then strained and bottled. Through the ages, many different "recipes" for cosmetic herbal vinegars have evolved. Floral vinegars, such as lavender, jasmine, rose, and pinks, are especially favored for tonics, but many of the more traditional culinary herbs are good for the skin as well. To begin, consider using one or a combination of the herbs in the list below or from the list of therapeutic herbs. (See pages 43–44.)

Basic Cosmetic Vinegar I (for the bath, face, or hair)

Mix together 2 ounces fresh or 1 ounce each of dried thyme leaves, lavender flowers, spearmint leaves, rosemary leaves, and sage leaves. Steep with 4 cups of apple cider vinegar or wine vinegar for several weeks, then strain. Mix together ¼ ounce gum camphor, ½ ounce gum benzoin, and 3 tablespoons grain alcohol until dissolved. Stir into vinegar, cover, and let stand for three days. Strain, bottle, cap tightly, and label.

Basic Cosmetic Vinegar II (for the bath, skin, or hair)

Mix together 2 ounces fresh or 1 ounce each of dried orange peel, leaves, and flowers, rose leaves, petals, and hips, willow bark, and chamomile flowers. Steep with 4 cups of apple cider or wine vinegar for several weeks, then strain. Add 1 cup rose water. Bottle, cap tightly, and label.

Herbal Vinegar Facial Tonic Combinations

Apple Cider Vinegar or Wine Vinegar	Orange peel, orange mint leaves, and calendula petals
	Lavender flowers, lady's mantle leaves, and rose petals
	Rose petals, chamomile flowers, and rose water
	Lavender flowers and rosemary, mint, and thyme leaves
	Lavender flowers and mint leaves
	Calendula petals and witch hazel

Baths

Adding either plain or herbal vinegar to bath water does for the entire body what vinegar skin tonics do for the face. Your skin responds favorably to having the proper acid, or pH balance. Vinegar in the bath water relaxes, soothes, cleanses, and removes itching, flaking skin. Use plain apple cider, rice, or wine vinegar or an herbal vinegar, adding ¼ to 1 cup vinegar to the bath water. (You can also add herbs to bath water separately by tying them up in a washcloth or muslin bath bag.) Herbal vinegars also make delightful after-bath body splashes for softening the skin; use full-strength or diluted.

Some preferred herbal mixtures for the bath, either infused in vinegar or added in bath bags, follow. Use fresh or dried herbs in whatever proportions you prefer.

Herbal Bath Combinations

Apple Cider Vinegar, Rice Vinegar, or Wine Vinegar	Orange peel, comfrey leaves, chamomile flowers, rose petals, and peppermint leaves
	Lavender flowers and rosemary leaves
	Spearmint leaves, almond oil, and witch hazel
	Bay, peppermint or spearmint, lemongrass, and comfrey leaves
	Sage, thyme, and savory leaves and lavender flowers
	Rose water, whole crushed cloves, and bay leaves
	Rose petals and chamomile flowers
	Orange peel, flowers, and leaves

Hair Rinses

After shampooing, rinsing your hair with vinegar leaves it squeaky clean and shining. Vinegar infused with different herbs can enhance different hair colors and condition hair as well. Rosemary and parsley are both good for dark hair, sage darkens greying hair, chamomile brings highlights to blonde or light brown hair, calendula provides conditioning, lavender and lemon verbena add fragrance, linden is good for frequently shampooed hair, and nettles condition hair and control dandruff.

Herbal Hair Rinse Combinations

Rosemary, sage, and southernwood leaves
Rosemary and mint leaves
Orange and lemon peels and mint and rosemary leaves
Chamomile and linden flowers and fennel, sage, rosemary, nettle, horsetail, and yarrow leaves

Other Cosmetic and Medicinal Uses for Vinegar

Dandruff. Massage full-strength vinegar into the scalp several times a week before shampooing.

Nail polish. Make nail polish more long-lasting by soaking fingertips in a solution of 2 teaspoons vinegar in ½ cup warm water for a minute before applying polish.

Douche. Although frequent douching is no longer generally recommended, women who are prone to vaginal infections can help prevent them by occasionally douching with a solution of 1 or 2 tablespoons of apple cider vinegar in a quart of warm water.

Acne. Make a mixture of 2 teaspoons of plain or herbal apple cider vinegar in 1 cup of water and dab on blemishes several times a day after washing. Old herbals recommend a mixture of onion and vinegar for blemishes.

Freckles. Lighten freckles on the body (not the face) by rubbing on horseradish vinegar. This is also said to repel mosquitoes.

Insect and Bee Stings. Repel insects before going outdoors by rubbing vinegar on your body, particularly the vulnerable wrists, hands, ankles, face, and throat. If bitten, dab apple cider vinegar on bites and stings as soon as possible to draw out the poison and prevent swelling. Thyme vinegar and rosemary vinegar are especially effective for both repelling insects and relieving discomfort from bites.

Toothache. Rub calendula or acacia vinegar for temporary relief.

Liniment. Use one of the herbal cosmetic vinegars as a pleasing alternative to alcohol as a rubbing lotion for aching muscles or for anyone confined to a bed. Apply to sprains as a hot poultice. Onion slices dipped in vinegar and rubbed on bruises immediately after they occur are said to prevent black-and-blue marks.

Headache Remedy. When you have a headache, dab an herbal toilet vinegar on your temples while resting. Alternatively, dampen a cloth with some of the vinegar and lay it across your brow.

Burns and Sunburn. To alleviate the pain of minor burns and sunburn, including lye burns, pat cold apple cider vinegar on affected area every 20 minutes or so.

Sore Throat and Fevers. Enhance the healing properties of chicken soup by adding 1 tablespoon vinegar, 1 crushed garlic clove, and a few drops of hot pepper sauce to a cup of hot chicken broth. Or, simply mix 1 tablespoon each of honey and apple cider vinegar or 2 tablespoons of sweetened raspberry or blackberry vinegar in a cup of hot water to promote rest, soothe a scratchy throat, and relieve congestion.

Chapped Skin. Chapped hands heal quickly when treated with a homemade mixture of equal parts rich hand cream and vinegar. Use it every time you wash your hands.

Athlete's Foot. Relieve the itching of athlete's foot by rinsing the feet several times a day with plain or herbal apple cider vinegar.

Corns. Soak two slices of white bread with 2 slices of onion and 1 cup of vinegar for 24 hours. Place bread on corn, top with a slice of the onion, then wrap with a bandage and leave on overnight.

Hiccups. Pliny suggested a small drink of chervil seed vinegar to cure hiccups.

Incontinence. Bathe with soap and water, then wipe the skin with vinegar. This reduces odor and lowers the pH of the skin, which helps prevent the growth of bacteria.

Morning Sickness. To relieve morning sickness, upon rising add a teaspoon of apple cider vinegar to a glass of water and drink it.

Physiological Effects of Stress and Chronic Fatigue. Chronic fatigue associated with a stressful lifestyle is due in part to the increase in blood pH. To reduce blood alkalinity, drink a glass of water with 2 teaspoons of apple cider vinegar first thing in the morning.

Sinusitis and Facial Neuralgia. Relieve the pain of sinusitis and facial neuralgia by drinking a glass of water with 1 teaspoon of apple cider vinegar added every hour for seven doses.

Indigestion. To reduce indigestion, add 2 teaspoons of apple cider vinegar to a glass of water and drink at each meal.

Arthritis. In his book, D. C. Jarvis, M.D., reports that drinking 2½ tablespoons of apple cider vinegar in a glass of water at each meal helps to alleviate arthritis.

Pet Health. To improve dog's or cat's health, add 1 tablespoon vinegar to pet's water.

Therapeutic Herbs

A number of herbs have been shown to contribute to general good health. You might consider using some of the following steeped in vinegar for the reason given.

Acacia /*Acacia* spp. Astringent, soothes and heals dry skin.

Bay /*Laurus nobilis.* Antiseptic, stimulates.

Burnet /*Poterium sanguisorba.* Softens, improves texture, astringent.

Calendula /*Calendula officinalis.* Astringent, soothes, softens, heals, clears blemishes, highlights blonde or brown hair.

Chamomile /*Chamaemelum nobile.* For normal skin, antiseptic, astringent, cleanses, softens, soothes, highlights blonde or brown hair.

Clover, red /*Trifolium pratense.* Soothes, heals.

Clover, yellow sweet /*Melilotus officinalis.* Treatment for dry skin, astringent, antibiotic, heals, soothes.

Colts foot /*Tussilago farfara.* Stimulates circulation; heals sores, throat problems.

Comfrey /*Symphytum officinale.* Heals, soothes, for burns and swellings, astringent.

Cucumber /*Cucumis sativus.* Treatment for oily skin, astringent.

Echinacea /*Echinacea angustifolia.* Antiseptic, heals, improves circulation.

Elder flowers /*Sambucus* spp. For dry skin, softens, heals, cleanses, whitens skin.

Eucalyptus /*Eucalyptus globulus.* Antiseptic, deodorant, stimulates, soothes, heals.

Fennel /*Foeniculum vulgare.* Cleanses, invigorates, astringent, smooths.

Honeysuckle /*Lonicera* spp. Antiseptic, astringent.

Horsetail /*Equisetum arvense.* Heals cuts and sores; antibiotic; mouthwash.

Juniper /*Juniperus communis.* Relieves sore muscles/joints, antiseptic, stimulates.

Lady's mantle /*Alchemilla vulgaris.* Treatment for dry skin, cleanses, heals, astringent, lightens freckles.

Lavender /*Lavandula angustifolia.* Treatment for oily skin, stimulates, antiseptic, relieves joint pain.

Lemon balm /*Melissa officinalis.* Soothes, astringent, cleanses, smooths.

Lemon peel /*Citrus limon.* Treatment for oily skin, stimulates, astringent, tonic.

Lemon verbena /*Aloysia triphylla.* Stimulates.

Linden /*Tilia cordata.* Cleanses, smooths, soothes, stimulates, improves circulation, slight bleaching action.

Lovage /*Levistichum officinale.* Cleanses, deodorizes.

Marjoram /*Origanum majorana.* Antiseptic, relieves fatigue, heals, soothes, relieves sore throat and aching muscles and joints.

Mint /*Mentha* spp. For normal skin, refreshes, cools, heals, stimulates, astringent, relieves headaches.

Myrrh /*Commiphoramolmol.* Antiseptic, astringent, heals/soothes sore throat.

Nettle /*Urtica* spp. Treatment for oily skin, astringent, cleanses, stimulates circulation, conditions hair, controls dandruff.

Orange /*Citrus* spp. Treatment for dry skin, soothes.

Oregano /*Oregano vulgare.* Antiseptic, heals, soothes, relieves sore throat and aching muscles and joints.

Parsley /*Petroselinum crispum.* For oily skin, cleanses, lightens freckles, adds shine to dark hair.

Plantain /*Plantago major.* Cleanses, astringent, soothes, heals.

Rose /*Rosa* spp. For normal skin, astringent, hydrates, heals, soothes.

Rosemary /*Rosmarinus officinalis.* For oily skin, stimulates, invigorates, gives shine and body to dark hair, antiseptic, insect repellent, soothes, heals.

Rue /*Ruta graveolens.* Stimulates, heals, soothes, relieves muscle and joint pain.

Sage /*Salvia officinalis.* For oily skin, stimulates, strong astringent, conditions dark hair, relieves aching muscles.

Sorrel /*Rumex acetosa.* Antiseptic, soothes, heals, dries.

Southernwood /*Artemisia abrotanum.* Antiseptic, heals, soothes.

Thyme /*Thymus* spp. Antiseptic, stimulates, deodorizes.

Violet /*Viola* spp. Clears blemishes, stimulates, heals, soothes.

Willow /*Salix alba.* Disinfectant, astringent, relieves muscle and joint pain and fevers and chills.

Wormwood /*Artemisia absinthium.* Antiseptic, relieves joint and muscle pain.

Yarrow /*Achillea millefolium.* For oily skin, astringent, cleanses, improves circulations, heals, relieves joint and muscle pain, reduces fever.

VINEGAR IN COOKING

s one of the oldest known flavoring staples, vinegar's current resurgence in popularity is no surprise to cooks who have long savored its tangy, refreshing nuances of flavor. One of the keys to good cooking, vinegar deepens the taste of any dish, adding a sharp, clean dimension. Its aroma harmonizes well with herbs and other ingredients, too. Most important to us in the late-twentieth century is that by adding vinegar to a dish, we have a healthy, calorie-conscious alternative to rich sauces and salty foods. Whether making a spinach salad with shallot-flavored vinegar, using cilantro rice vinegar in delicate Asian concoctions, poaching duck breasts in a raspberry vinegar, or dressing oysters in a tarragon vinegar mignonette sauce, vinegar's bracing jolt of flavor has a sublime influence.

The recipes I've included in this book merely scratch the surface of the many ways that vinegar can be used in cooking. I encourage you to experiment. Be willing to add a bit of vinegar to sauces and gravies, grilled meats, steamed or sautéed vegetables, pasta sauces, and even desserts and beverages.

SUBSTITUTIONS

Although I've suggested specifically flavored vinegars in these recipes, if you don't have a particular one available, try the dish with a plain vinegar or another flavor. If you don't have the fresh herbs called for in these recipes, substitute dried herbs, at half the recommended amount.

Tips for Using Vinegar in the Kitchen

Buttermilk substitute. To substitute for buttermilk in a recipe, add 1 tablespoon vinegar to a cup of fresh or canned evaporated milk, then let it stand for 5 minutes before using.

Store pimiento peppers. An opened jar of canned pimiento peppers can be kept for weeks if they are covered with vinegar and refrigerated.

Prevent mold on cheese. Keep cheese soft and mold-free by wrapping it in a cloth saturated with vinegar, then storing it in an airtight container in the refrigerator.

Store herbs. Instead of drying herbs, try storing them in vinegar. Loosely pack a scalded jar with fresh herbs, add warmed vinegar to cover by one inch, making sure all leaves are immersed, then cover tightly. Herbs can be stored at room temperature and used in the same proportion as dried herbs. This works especially well with tarragon and white wine vinegar.

Keep ginger fresh. Peel ginger and grate or process in a food processor. Fill a clean jar and cover with sherry or balsamic vinegar. Store in refrigerator.

Garlic substitute. Use garlic wine vinegar in place of fresh garlic in any recipe. A teaspoon is the equivalent of a small clove of garlic.

Improve soups and tomato sauce. One or two tablespoons of vinegar added to soups or tomato sauces in the last five minutes of cooking enhances their flavors.

Substitute vinegar for wine. When a recipe calls for wine, substitute vinegar, diluting one part of vinegar with three parts of water.

Salvage over-salted food. Food that has been oversalted can be rescued by adding a teaspoon each of vinegar and sugar, then reheating.

Mold-less canning jars. To prevent mold on the outside of canning jars, wipe jars with vinegar after they are sealed.

Mayonnaise retrieval. Get the last remaining contents of mayonnaise or salad dressing out of the jars by adding a bit of vinegar and shaking.

Clean fruits and vegetables. Wash fruits and vegetables in water with vinegar added to remove pesticides, heavy metal residues, and insects. Use 2½ tablespoons of vinegar to a gallon of water.

Revive wilted vegetables. Freshen vegetables that are slightly wilted in a cold water-vinegar solution.

Better steamed vegetables. Retain bright color and vitamin content of vegetables by adding 2 teaspoons of vinegar to the water for steaming. This also prevents off-odors.

Keep fruits and vegetables from discoloring. Keep potatoes from turning black or apples and avocadoes from browning by tossing cut up pieces with vinegar or adding one or two teaspoons of vinegar to the cooking water or water they're kept in until ready for use in recipes.

Better mashed potatoes. After the last of the hot milk has been added to mashed potatoes, add a teaspoon of vinegar and beat them a little more.

Improve fried foods. Make fried foods seem less greasy by adding a tablespoon of vinegar to the deep fryer or skillet before adding the oil.

Tenderize meats. Marinate meats in herb-flavored wine vinegar to tenderize them. The sourness cooks away, leaving the flavor of the herbs and wine.

Better hamburgers. Add a teaspoon of garlic wine vinegar and ½ teaspoon mustard to a pound of hamburger.

Boiled beef. Improve the taste and texture of boiled beef by adding 1 or more tablespoons of vinegar to the cooking water.

Boiled ham. Improve the flavor of boiled ham by adding vinegar to the cooking water.

Improve flavor of wild game. To remove the gamey flavor from wild meat, soak the meat in a vinegar-water solution before cooking.

Cleaning fish. Before scaling fish, rub with vinegar to make scaling easier and keep hands from smelling fishy.

Better fish. Add a tablespoon or more of vinegar to fried or boiled fish when cooking. To keep fish white, soak the fish for 20 minutes in a mixture of 1 quart water and 2 tablespoons vinegar.

Better hard-cooked eggs. Eggs that are cracked can be hard-cooked without the white running out by adding vinegar to the boiling water.

Well-shaped poached eggs. To poach eggs, put a saucepan of water on medium-high heat, add 2 teaspoons of vinegar, and bring to a simmer. Crack an egg into a cup. With a wooden spoon, briskly stir the water, creating a whirlpool. Pour the egg into the vortex. Cook for 2 minutes.

Shiny homemade bread. Add a sheen to the crust of homemade bread by brushing the top of bread with vinegar several minutes before done, then returning it to the oven to complete baking.

Better-rising bread. To help bread rise, add 1 tablespoon of vinegar for every 2½ cups flour when adding other liquids, reducing those liquids accordingly. This makes the gluten more elastic. The same technique also makes struedel dough more pliant.

Fluffy, stable meringue. Make fluffier, more stable meringue by adding vinegar in the proportion of ½ teaspoon of vinegar to three egg whites.

Seven-minute frosting. To keep seven-minute frosting white and soft, add ½ teaspoon vinegar to a recipe calling for 1½ cups sugar and 2 egg whites.

Firmer gelatin. To keep gelatin firmer in warm weather, add a teaspoon of vinegar.

Better desserts. Add a teaspoon of vinegar to pies and other desserts to enhance flavor and reduce cloying sweetness.

APPETIZERS

SPICED PICKLED EGGS

Yield: 12 eggs

     12 small eggs, hard-cooked and peeled
      1 small onion, thinly sliced
      3 cups mixed-spice red wine vinegar
         One 3-inch cinnamon stick
      1 tablespoon honey
      1 teaspoon whole allspice
      1 teaspoon whole cloves
      ½ teaspoon whole coriander seeds
      1 quarter-size slice fresh ginger
      1 bayleaf

Place eggs and onion in a wide-mouth jar. Combine remaining ingredients in a nonreactive saucepan over medium heat. Bring the mixture to a boil, reduce heat to low, and simmer for 5 minutes. Pour over the eggs. Cover and refrigerate for a week before serving. Eggs will keep about two months in the refrigerator.

Variations. Try garlic-purple basil vinegar, or substitute carnation vinegar or cinnamon basil vinegar and use only cloves and cinnamon for the spices.

PICKLED EGGS

Pickled eggs are traditionally made with malt vinegar and served in English pubs as an accompaniment to a ploughman's lunch of bread, cheese, pickled onions, and cold cuts. They also serve well halved and made into deviled eggs, sliced thinly and served on toast triangles, and quartered or sliced and added to mixed green, potato, pasta, or tuna salads. Experiment with a variety of vinegars and herbs or spices as well as other vegetables besides beets. Add or subtract ingredients as taste and whim dictate. Some people like to add a teaspoon of salt to the mixture.

Fresh Herb Pickled Eggs

Yield: 12 eggs

12 small eggs, hard-cooked and peeled
¼ cup shallots, thinly sliced
2 sprigs fresh thyme
2 sprigs fresh marjoram
2 sprigs fresh parsley
1 clove garlic
1 small hot red pepper or
1 teaspoon whole black peppercorns
3 cups mixed-herb white wine or rice vinegar
1 tablespoon honey

Place eggs, shallots, herbs, garlic, and pepper or peppercorns in a wide-mouth jar. Stir honey into vinegar and pour over the eggs. Cover and refrigerate for a week before serving. Eggs will keep about two months in the refrigerator.

Variations. Consider substituting other vinegar flavors, especially raspberry, tarragon, thyme, dill, basil, or garlic chives. Also substitute fresh herbs as desired.

Pickled Herring

The classic way to serve these is by first buttering a thin slice of rye or pumpernickle bread, then adding a leaf of butter head lettuce and several pieces of drained marinated herring. Add some onion rings from the marinade, chopped capers, radishes, chives, parsley, or dill, a lemon slice, and a dollop of sour cream or crème fraîche.

Yield: 1 pound

1 pound salt-cured herring
Cold water or buttermilk
1 medium red onion, thinly sliced and separated into rings
2 cups mixed-herb or spice white wine or cider vinegar
½ cup water
⅓ cup sugar
1 teaspoon whole black peppercorns
1 teaspoon whole allspice
1 teaspoon mustard seeds

½ teaspoon whole cloves

1 small hot red pepper (optional)

2 bay leaves

Rinse herring under running cold water. Slit the bellies and remove the innards. Place in a shallow nonreactive dish and cover with cold water or buttermilk. Cover and refrigerate overnight. Drain and rinse under running cold water. Remove tails, fins, and back bones, if desired. Slice crosswise into 1-inch pieces.

In a wide-mouth quart jar, alternate layers of herring and onion. In a nonreactive saucepan, combine vinegar, sugar, peppercorns, allspice, mustard seeds, cloves, bay leaves, and hot pepper. Bring to a boil over medium heat, then reduce heat to low and simmer for 5 minutes. Let cool and pour over the herring and onions, cover, and refrigerate for at least 24 hours.

This keeps for at least two months.

Variations. Substitute salt-cured but unsmoked salmon, also called lox or belly lox, cutting off the skin after soaking. Pickling spices may be substituted. Or, add ½ teaspoon each coriander, cumin, and dill seeds to the spices above.

Marinated Shrimp

Yield: 8 servings

¾ cup chive blossom white wine or rice vinegar

¾ cup extra-virgin olive oil

¼ cup shallots, minced

¼ cup sweet green pepper, cored, seeded, and minced

2 tablespoons fresh chives, minced

1 tablespoon Dijon mustard

1 tablespoon capers

1 clove garlic, minced

½ teaspoon hot red pepper sauce

4 pounds shrimp, peeled and deveined

In a large nonreactive bowl, combine all ingredients except shrimp. Whisk together.

Fill a large kettle three-fourths full of water and bring to a boil over high heat. Add shrimp and cook until opaque in the center, or about 3 to 4 minutes. Drain and add to the marinade, stirring to coat. Cover and refrigerate for at least 3 or 4 hours before serving.

CHEESE-NUT BALL

Yield: 2½ cups

- 8 ounces low-fat Swiss-style cheese, grated
- 3 ounces low-fat cream cheese
- ¾ cup pecans, finely chopped
- ½ cup apple, cored, peeled, and grated
- 3 tablespoons sage cider vinegar
- 3 tablespoons fresh sage, minced

In a mixer or food processor, mix together the two cheeses, ½ cup pecans, apple, vinegar, and sage. Add additional vinegar if mixture seems too dry. Form entire mixture into a ball and roll it in remaining pecans. Cover and refrigerate for several hours before serving.

PICKLED SALMON

Yield: 2 pounds

- 1 cup unbleached all-purpose flour
- 1 teaspoon salt
- ½ teaspoon freshly ground black pepper
- 2 pounds salmon fillets, cut into 2-inch squares
- ⅓ cup extra-virgin olive oil
- 2 medium onions, thinly sliced
- 2 medium carrots, thinly sliced
- 2 cloves garlic, minced
- 1 teaspoon fresh marjoram, minced
- 1 bay leaf, crumbled
- 1 small hot red pepper
- 1 cup marjoram white wine vinegar
- ¼ cup water

In a bowl, combine the flour, salt, and pepper. Dredge the salmon in the flour mixture and shake off the excess. Warm the oil in a heavy nonreactive skillet over medium-high heat and sauté the fish on both sides until lightly browned, or about 3 to 5 minutes. Remove to a shallow nonreactive dish.

Add the onions and carrots to the skillet and cook over medium heat, stirring, for 5 minutes. Add garlic and cook, stirring, for 30 seconds. Stir in the marjoram, bay leaf, hot pepper, vinegar, and water, bring to a simmer, and cook for 5 minutes. Pour the vegetable mixture over the salmon, cover, and refrigerate for at least 24 hours before serving.

Variations. Mackerel, shad, or other firm oily fish can be substituted for the salmon.

Cucumber-Cheese Dip

Yield: 2 cups

- 1 medium cucumber, peeled, seeded, and diced
- 2 tablespoons burnet white wine or rice vinegar
- 2 tablespoons fresh burnet, minced
- 2 tablespoons fresh dill, minced
- 1 clove garlic, minced
- 1 teaspoon salt
- ½ teaspoon freshly ground black pepper
- 1 cup low-fat or nonfat ricotta cheese
- ½ cup nonfat plain yogurt

In a nonreactive bowl, combine cucumber, vinegar, burnet, dill, garlic, salt, and pepper. Stir in the ricotta and yogurt, adding more vinegar if necessary to get the desired consistency. Cover and refrigerate for at least several hours before serving.

Olive-Roasted Pepper-Eggplant Dip

Yield: 1 cup

- 1 cup imported black olives, pitted and chopped
- 1 cup sweet red pepper, roasted, peeled, cored, seeded, and chopped
- 1 cup eggplant, roasted, peeled, and chopped
- 2 green onions, chopped
- 1 small tomato, peeled, seeded, and diced
- 3 tablespoons extra-virgin olive oil
- 3 tablespoons basil or thyme red wine or sherry vinegar
- 1 tablespoon fresh basil, minced
- 1 tablespoon fresh thyme, minced
- 1 tablespoon fresh parsley, minced

In a blender or food processor, combine all ingredients until just blended. The dip should still have some recognizable pieces.

Herb-Cheese Spread

Yield: 2 cups

  4 ounces Monterey jack cheese, grated
  4 ounces blue cheese, crumbled
  3 ounces low-fat cream cheese, at room temperature
  2 ounces Parmesan cheese, grated
  ¾ cup reduced-calorie mayonnaise
  ¼ cup low-fat or nonfat sour cream
  ½ cup mixed-herb sherry vinegar
  ¼ cup fresh parsley, minced
  ¼ cup green onions, minced
  2 tablespoons fresh basil, minced
  2 tablespoons fresh chives, minced

In a nonreactive bowl, combine all ingredients. Arrange in a mound on a serving platter or bowl, cover, and refrigerate for several hours before serving.

CHAPTER 7

MAIN COURSES AND SOUPS

CHICKEN BREASTS IN VINEGAR-CREAM SAUCE

Yield: 4 servings

- 2 pounds skinless, boneless chicken breasts
  Salt and freshly ground black pepper to taste
- 3 tablespoons canola oil
- 4 cloves garlic, minced
- 3 tablespoons fresh thyme, minced
- 3 tablespoons fresh marjoram, minced
- ⅔ cup thyme or mixed herb red wine vinegar
- ½ cup vegetable stock or water
- 3 tablespoons sun-dried tomatoes, minced
- ⅓ cup low-fat or nonfat sour cream
  Fresh thyme and marjoram

Sprinkle the chicken breasts with salt and pepper. Heat the oil over medium heat in a large heavy nonreactive skillet. Add the chicken and cook on both sides until golden. Add the garlic and cook until soft, being careful not to burn. Sprinkle in the thyme and marjoram, cover the pan, reduce heat to low, and cook for 15 minutes, or until the chicken breasts are cooked through. Remove the chicken to a serving platter and keep warm. Increase the heat to medium and pour in the vinegar, scraping the bottom to loosen any bits. Add the stock or water and the dried tomato. Stirring constantly, cook the sauce until reduced by half. Remove from heat and stir in the sour cream. Pour the sauce over the chicken and sprinkle with fresh minced herbs.

GRILLED CHICKEN BREASTS MARINATED IN VINEGAR-MUSTARD SAUCE

Yield: 4 servings

- ½ cup herb mustard, preferably a Dijon-type
- ½ cup mixed herb white wine vinegar
- ½ cup extra-virgin olive oil
- 4–6 cloves garlic
- 1 teaspoon fresh rosemary
- 1 teaspoon fresh thyme
- 1 teaspoon fresh marjoram
- 1 teaspoon fresh basil
- 1 teaspoon fresh sage
- 1 teaspoon fresh savory
- 1 teaspoon fresh fennel
- 1 teaspoon fresh lavender
- 3 pounds chicken breasts

Combine all ingredients except chicken in a blender or food processor until smooth. Place chicken pieces in a shallow nonreactive dish and pour the marinade over the top. Cover, refrigerate, and marinate overnight, or for at least 4 hours. Remove the chicken from the marinade and grill it over medium-hot coals until cooked through, basting as needed with remaining marinade.

CURRIED CHICKEN

Yield: 4 servings

- 2 tablespoons butter
- 1 tablespoon canola oil
- 2 medium onions, thinly sliced
- 2 cloves garlic, minced
- 2 teaspoons fresh ginger, minced
- 4 medium tomatoes, peeled, seeded, and chopped
- 2 potatoes, peeled and diced
- ½ cup sweet green pepper, cored, seeded, and diced
- ¼ cup spice or cilantro white wine vinegar
- 2 tablespoons water
- 2 tablespoons tomato paste
- 1 tablespoon anchovy paste

2 teaspoons ground coriander seeds

1 teaspoon ground cayenne pepper

1 teaspoon ground cumin seeds

1 teaspoon garam masala or curry powder

½ teaspoon turmeric

¼ teaspoon ground cloves

2 pounds skinless, boneless chicken breast, cut into 1-inch pieces

Warm the butter and oil in a large, heavy nonreactive skillet over medium heat. Add the onion, garlic, and ginger and sauté until golden, stirring constantly and being careful not to let it brown. After about 5 minutes, or when the onion is softened, stir in the tomatoes, potatoes, green pepper, vinegar, water, tomato paste, anchovy paste, coriander, cayenne, cumin, garam masala or curry powder, tumeric, and cloves. Bring to a boil, reduce heat to low, cover, and simmer for 20 minutes. Add chicken and stir to coat. Replace cover and cook for 10 minutes, or until chicken is cooked through. Serve with dishes of chutney, chopped peanuts, currants, and grated unsweetened coconut.

JAMAICAN BARBECUED CHICKEN BREASTS

Yield: 4 servings

8 green onions, chopped

¼ cup garlic red wine vinegar

2 tablespoons canola oil

1 tablespoon soy sauce

2 teaspoons ground allspice

1 fresh green jalapeño or habañero pepper, cored and seeded

½ teaspoon freshly ground black pepper

½ teaspoon ground cinnamon

¼ teaspoon ground nutmeg

4 skinless, boneless chicken breast halves

Combine onions, vinegar, oil, soy sauce, allspice, hot pepper, black pepper, cinnamon, and nutmeg in a blender or food processor and puree. Pour puree into a shallow nonreactive dish. Add chicken breasts, turning to coat. Cover and refrigerate for 4 hours, turning occasionally. Remove chicken from marinade and grill over medium-hot coals until cooked through, or about 20 minutes, turning several times.

Spicy Beef Stew

Yield: 4 servings

  2 tablespoons canola oil

1½ pounds beef chuck, cut into 1-inch pieces

  ½ cup mixed-spice red wine vinegar

  ⅓ cup tomato sauce

  3 medium tomatoes, peeled, seeded, and chopped

  1 tablespoon honey

  1 teaspoon salt

  2 cloves garlic, minced

  1 teaspoon fresh rosemary, minced

  ½ teaspoon ground cinnamon

  ½ teaspoon ground cumin seeds

  ½ teaspoon freshly ground black pepper

  ¼ teaspoon ground cloves

  1 bay leaf

  1 cup water

1½ pounds pearl onions, peeled

  ¼ cup fresh parsley, minced

Preheat oven to 300°F. In a heavy ovenproof nonreactive casserole, warm the oil over medium-high heat. Add the beef and brown on all sides. Add the vinegar, tomato sauce, tomatoes, honey, salt, garlic, rosemary, cinnamon, cumin, black pepper, cloves, and bay leaf and stir. Add the water, onions, and parsley. Cover and bring to a boil, then place in oven. Bake for 1 hour, or until the meat is tender, adding water if necessary. Remove bay leaf before serving.

Lamb Stew with Fennel Sauce

Yield: 4 servings

  2 pounds lean, boneless lamb, cut into 1-inch cubes

  2 tablespoons canola oil

  2 cups beef or vegetable stock, or water, boiling

  1 cup fennel vinegar

  3 tablespoons fresh fennel, minced

  1 teaspoon salt

½ teaspoon freshly ground black pepper

2 tablespoons butter

2 tablespoons unbleached all-purpose flour

2 cups beef or vegetable stock

1½ tablespoons fennel vinegar

1 large egg yolk, beaten until lemon-colored

Heat oil in a large, heavy nonreactive pan over medium heat. Add lamb cubes and cook until browned on all sides. Add boiling stock or water, vinegar, 1 tablespoon fennel, salt, and pepper. Bring to a boil, reduce heat to low, cover, and simmer for 1 hour, or until tender.

About 15 minutes before the lamb is done, prepare the sauce. In a heavy, nonreactive saucepan, melt butter over medium heat and stir in flour until smooth. Add stock gradually, stirring constantly to keep the mixture smooth. Reduce heat and cook for 10 minutes, stirring occasionally. Remove from heat and stir in remaining fennel, vinegar, and egg yolk. When lamb is tender, drain and place on a platter and serve with sauce and egg noodles or boiled new potatoes.

PORK WITH APPLES AND SAGE

Yield: 4 servings

1½ pounds boneless pork cutlets

3 tablespoons unbleached all-purpose flour

Salt and freshly ground black pepper to taste

2 tablespoons canola oil

2 apples, cored and thinly sliced

1 medium onion, thinly sliced

2 tablespoons fresh sage, minced

2 cloves garlic, minced

1 cup sage cider vinegar

Preheat oven to 350°F. Combine flour with salt and pepper to taste. Lightly dredge pork in flour. Heat oil in a heavy skillet over medium heat. Fry the pork until golden on both sides. Layer the pork with apples, onion, garlic, and sage in a heavy nonreactive ovenproof casserole. Pour the vinegar over the top and cover. Bake for 1 hour.

Garlic Pork

Yield: 4 servings

- ¼ pound garlic cloves
- 1 tablespoon fresh thyme
- 2 fresh hot red peppers, cored and seeded
- 1 cup thyme white wine or rice vinegar
- 1 cup water
- 1 teaspoon salt
- ¼ teaspoon ground cloves
- 2 pounds pork loin, cut into 1-inch pieces
- 1 tablespoon canola oil

Combine garlic cloves, thyme, and hot peppers in a blender or food processor until well blended. Add vinegar, water, salt, and cloves and blend. Place the pork in a nonreactive bowl and pour the vinegar mixture over the top. Cover the bowl and refrigerate for 3 days. Warm a heavy nonreactive skillet over medium heat and add the pork mixture. Cook until the liquid evaporates, then add the oil and fry for an additional 5 minutes.

Sautéed Trout with Vinegar Sauce

Yield: 4 servings

- ¼ cup unbleached all-purpose flour
- 1 teaspoon salt
- ½ teaspoon freshly ground black pepper
- 4 rainbow trout
  Four 4-inch sprigs of fresh rosemary
- 1 tablespoon fresh lemon zest, minced
- 3 tablespoons extra-virgin olive oil
- 2 cloves garlic, minced
- ¼ cup rosemary white wine or rice vinegar
- ¼ cup dry vermouth

Combine the flour, salt, and pepper. Lightly coat each trout with some of the flour mixture, shaking to remove excess flour. Place a sprig of rosemary and some of the lemon zest inside each trout. Warm the oil in a heavy nonreactive skillet on medium heat and sauté the trout on each side until golden and fish flakes easily. Remove and place on a platter. Add garlic to the skillet and 1 tablespoon of the seasoned flour. Stirring constantly, cook until the garlic and flour are golden. Continuing to stir, pour in the vinegar and vermouth and cook until slightly thickened. Pour sauce over the fish.

MONKFISH WITH LEMON HERB VINEGAR SAUCE

Yield: 4 servings

- 3 tablespoons extra-virgin olive oil
- 3 cloves garlic, minced
- 1½ pounds monkfish, cut into 1-inch pieces
- 2 tablespoons fresh lemon thyme, minced
- Freshly ground black pepper to taste
- 3 tablespoons lemon thyme white wine or rice vinegar

Warm the oil in a large heavy nonreactive skillet over medium-high heat. Add the garlic and cook until golden, stirring constantly and being careful not to let it brown. Add the fish, lemon thyme, and pepper to taste. When the fish is cooked through, add the vinegar, heat to a simmer, and serve.

TOMATO AND BASIL SOUP

Yield: 4 servings

- 1 pound tomatoes, peeled, seeded, and diced
- 1 medium onion, chopped
- ¾ pound potatoes, peeled and diced
- 3 cups vegetable stock
- ⅓ cup basil or lemon basil white wine or rice vinegar
- ¼ cup fresh basil or lemon basil, minced
- 1 teaspoon salt
- ½ teaspoon freshly ground black pepper

In a large nonreactive saucepan, combine tomatoes, onion, potatoes, stock and vinegar. Cover and place over medium heat. Bring to a boil, reduce heat to low, and simmer for 30 minutes, or until potatoes are very soft. Pour the soup into a blender and puree. Stir in the basil, salt, and pepper.

Variation. Dill vinegar and fresh dill may be substituted for the dill vinegar and fresh dill.

Stir-Fried Shrimp and Broccoli with Ginger-Vinegar Sauce

Yield: 4 servings

     4 tablespoons ginger rice wine vinegar
     5 green onions, cut into 1-inch pieces
    16 paper-thin slices fresh ginger
     2 teaspoons garlic, minced
    1½ pounds shrimp, peeled and deveined
     1 pound fresh broccoli, cut into florets
    ⅓ cup vegetable broth
     2 teaspoons cornstarch
    1½ teaspoons toasted hot pepper sesame oil
     1 teaspoon soy sauce
     1 teaspoon sugar
    ¼ teaspoon hot red pepper sauce
     2 tablespoons untoasted sesame oil

In a nonreactive bowl, combine 2 tablespoons vinegar, 10 pieces of green onion, 4 slices of ginger, and 1 teaspoon garlic. Press with a spoon to release flavors; remove from the bowl. Add shrimp, stirring to coat; marinate for 30 minutes.

Bring a saucepan of salted water to a boil over medium-high heat and add the broccoli. Cook for 2½ minutes, drain, run under cold water, and drain again. Set broccoli aside.

In a nonreactive bowl, combine broth, cornstarch, hot pepper oil, soy sauce, sugar, hot pepper sauce, and remaining 2 tablespoons vinegar. Set aside.

Place a wok or heavy skillet over high heat and add untoasted sesame oil. Add the remaining green onions, ginger, and garlic and stir-fry for 20 seconds. Add the broccoli, toss, and cook for 1 minute. Add the shrimp, toss, and cook for 1 minute. Stir the broth mixture, add it to the wok, and cook, stirring, for 2 minutes, or until the sauce is thickened. Serve with rice.

Hot-and-Sour Soup

Yield: 4 servings

  6 dried cloud's ears or shiitake mushrooms
      Hot water
  4 cups vegetable stock
  8 ounces extra-firm tofu, cut into ½-inch pieces
  ½ cup bamboo shoots
  1 tablespoon soy sauce
  1 tablespoon toasted sesame oil
  ⅓ cup garlic or hot pepper sherry or rice vinegar
  2 tablespoons cornstarch
  3 tablespoons water
  1 large egg, beaten
  2 green onions, thinly sliced

In a bowl, pour hot water to cover over dried mushrooms. Let soak for 30 minutes. Drain, reserving the liquid. Slice the mushrooms, discarding the stalks and hard centers. In a large nonreactive saucepan, combine the reserved mushroom liquid, stock, sliced mushrooms, tofu, bamboo shoots, and soy sauce. Place over medium-high heat and simmer for 15 minutes. Stir in the oil and vinegar. In a small bowl, combine cornstarch and water, blending well. Stir the mixture into the soup. Continue to heat and stir until the soup is slightly thickened. Drizzle the beaten egg into the soup while stirring so that it forms thin strands. Serve garnished with the chopped green onion.

CHAPTER 8

Pastas, Grains, and Beans

Sesame Noodles

Yield: 4 servings

  8 ounces dry linguine
  3 tablespoons sesame oil
  ½ cup green onions, thinly sliced
  ¼ cup sesame seeds, toasted and crushed
  ¼ cup fresh cilantro, minced
  ¼ cup hot pepper red wine vinegar
  1 tablespoon fresh ginger, minced
  1 teaspoon honey
  ½ teaspoon hot red pepper sauce
  1 clove garlic, minced
    Salt and freshly ground black pepper to taste

Cook pasta until *al dente,* drain, rinse under cold water, and drain thoroughly. Place in a large shallow nonreactive bowl. Mix with 1 tablespoon sesame oil.

    In a small nonreactive bowl, whisk together remaining ingredients. Pour dressing over pasta mixture and toss until all ingredients are coated. Cover and refrigerate for several hours before serving to allow flavors to blend.

Vegetarian Baked Beans

Yield: 4 servings

- ½ pound dry pinto beans
- 2 tablespoons canola oil
- 1 cup onion, chopped
- 2 cloves garlic, minced
- 1 tablespoon fresh ginger, minced
- 1 jalapeño pepper, cored, seeded, and minced
- 1½ cups apple cider
- ½ cup mixed-herb or mixed-spice apple cider vinegar
- 2 tablespoons molasses
- 2 tablespoons packed light brown sugar
- 1 tablespoon Dijon mustard
- 1 bay leaf
- 1 tablespoon fresh thyme, minced
- Salt and freshly ground black pepper to taste

Rinse beans, place in a large bowl, and cover with cold water. Let sit overnight, or at least 8 hours. Drain and put into a nonreactive ovenproof casserole.

Preheat oven to 350° F. In a heavy nonreactive skillet, warm the oil over medium heat. Add the onion, garlic, and jalapeño pepper. Sauté until softened, or about 5 minutes, stirring occasionally. Stir into the beans with the remaining ingredients. Cover and bake until beans are tender, or about 2 to 3 hours.

Black Bean Salad

Yield: 4 to 6 servings

- Two 15- or 16-ounce cans black beans, drained and rinsed
- 1 cup cherry tomatoes, stemmed and quartered
- ½ cup green onions, thinly sliced
- ½ cup corn, cooked
- ½ cup sweet red pepper, cored, seeded, and diced
- ½ cup sweet yellow pepper, cored, seeded, and diced
- 2 tablespoons jalapeño pepper, cored, seeded, and diced
- ¼ cup fresh cilantro, minced
- ¼ cup marjoram sherry vinegar

2 tablespoons extra-virgin olive oil

2 tablespoons dry sherry

1 tablespoon fresh marjoram, minced

1 teaspoon coarse-grain mustard

½ teaspoon ground cumin seeds

½ teaspoon hot red pepper sauce

Salt and freshly ground black pepper to taste

In a large nonreactive bowl, combine beans, cherry tomatoes, green onions, corn, red and yellow sweet peppers, jalapeño peppers, and cilantro.

In a small nonreactive bowl, whisk together the vinegar, olive oil, sherry, marjoram, mustard, cumin, hot pepper sauce, salt, and pepper. Pour over the bean mixture and toss until all ingredients are coated. Cover and refrigerate for several hours before serving to allow flavors to blend.

Three-Bean Salad

Yield: 6 servings

½ pound green beans, trimmed, cut into 1-inch pieces, and cooked

One 15- or 16-ounce can pinto beans, drained and rinsed

One 16- or 19-ounce can garbanzo beans (chickpeas), drained and rinsed

1 cup mushrooms, sliced

½ cup sweet red pepper, roasted, peeled, cored, seeded, and diced

1 small sweet onion, thinly sliced

3 tablespoons savory white wine vinegar

2 tablespoons canola oil

¼ cup fresh summer savory, minced

¼ cup fresh parsley, minced

Salt and freshly ground black pepper to taste

In a large nonreactive bowl, combine the green beans, pinto beans, garbanzo beans, mushrooms, red pepper, and onion.

In a small bowl, whisk together the vinegar, oil, savory, parsley, salt, and pepper. Pour over the bean mixture and toss until all ingredients are coated. Cover and refrigerate for several hours before serving to allow flavors to blend.

White Bean Salad

Yield: 6 to 8 servings

> Two 15- or 16-ounce cans Great Northern beans,
> rinsed and drained
>
> ½ cup green onions, thinly sliced
> ¼ cup fresh basil, minced
> ¼ cup imported black olives, pitted and chopped
> ¼ cup sun-dried tomatoes, minced
> ¼ cup basil white wine vinegar
> 3 tablespoons extra-virgin olive oil
> 1 teaspoon Dijon mustard
> Salt and freshly ground black pepper to taste

In a nonreactive bowl, combine beans, green onions, basil, olives, and tomatoes. In a small nonreactive bowl, whisk together the vinegar, olive oil, mustard, and salt and pepper to taste. Pour over the bean mixture and toss. Cover and refrigerate for several hours to allow flavors to blend. Serve chilled or at room temperature.

Red Bean and Rice Salad

Yield: 4 servings

> ½ pound smoked low-fat turkey sausage in casings
> 1 cup plus 3 tablespoons garlic red wine vinegar
> One 15- or 16-ounce can red beans, drained and rinsed
> 1 cup cooked brown rice
> ½ cup cucumber, peeled, seeded, and diced
> ½ cup sweet red pepper, cored, seeded, and diced
> ¼ cup celery, diced
> ¼ cup green onions, thinly sliced
> 1 tablespoon extra-virgin olive oil
> 2 teaspoons coarse-grain mustard
> 1 tablespoon fresh thyme, minced
> 1 clove garlic, minced
> ½ teaspoon hot red pepper sauce
> Salt and freshly ground black pepper to taste

Combine sausage and 1 cup vinegar in a nonreactive saucepan and bring to a boil over medium heat. Cover, reduce heat to low, and simmer for 5 minutes, or until sausage is cooked through. Remove sausage from vinegar, cut into 1-inch pieces, and set aside.

In a large nonreactive bowl, combine beans, rice, cucumber, sweet pepper, celery, green onions, and reserved sausage.

In a small nonreactive bowl, whisk together the 3 tablespoons of vinegar, oil, mustard, thyme, garlic, hot pepper sauce, salt, and pepper. Pour over the bean mixture and toss until all ingredients are coated. Cover and refrigerate for several hours before serving to allow flavors to blend.

SPICED RICE SALAD

Yield: 4 servings

1½ cups water
 1 teaspoon salt
 ¾ cup raw long-grain brown rice
 1 tablespoon fresh ginger, minced
 ½ cup dried currants
    Boiling water
 ¼ cup red onion, finely chopped
 ¼ cup pistachio nuts, toasted
 ¼ cup extra-virgin olive oil
 3 tablespoons spice sherry vinegar
 ½ teaspoon ground allspice
 ¼ teaspoon ground nutmeg
 ¼ teaspoon ground cinnamon
    Salt and freshly ground black pepper to taste

Combine water and salt in a saucepan and bring to a boil over medium-high heat. Stir in rice and ginger and return to a boil. Cover, reduce heat to low, and simmer 45 minutes, or until tender.

Place currants in a small bowl and cover with boiling water. Let sit for 20 minutes, then drain.

In a large nonreactive bowl, combine rice, currants, red onion, pistachios, olive oil, vinegar, allspice, nutmeg, cinnamon, salt, and pepper. Toss until all ingredients are coated. Cover and refrigerate for several hours before serving to allow flavors to blend.

Sweet-and-Sour White Beans

Yield: 3 to 4 servings

One 15- or 16-ounce can of Great Northern beans,
drained and rinsed

2 tablespoons packed light brown sugar

¼ cup lemon thyme white wine or rice vinegar

1 tablespoon fresh lemon thyme, minced

½ teaspoon freshly ground black pepper

In a nonreactive saucepan, combine all ingredients. Cook over medium heat for 10 minutes, or until heated through.

Summer Vegetable Rice Salad

Yield: 4 servings

2 cups long-grain brown rice, cooked

1 cup cherry tomatoes, stemmed and halved

½ cup peas, cooked

½ cup summer squash, diced

¼ cup green onions, thinly sliced

¼ cup celery, thinly sliced

¾ cup low-fat or nonfat sour cream

3 tablespoons herb vinegar

2 tablespoons fresh herbs to match the vinegar,
such as dill, basil, parsley, thyme, chives,
garlic chives, or tarragon, minced

In a large nonreactive bowl combine the rice, tomatoes, peas, squash, onions, and celery.

In a small nonreactive bowl, combine remaining ingredients. Pour over rice mixture and toss until all ingredients are coated. Cover and refrigerate for several hours before serving to allow flavors to blend.

Barley Salad

Yield: 4 servings

1½ cups barley, cooked
⅓ cup sweet green pepper, cored, seeded, and diced
⅓ cup sweet red pepper, cored, seeded, and diced
1 cup corn, cooked
¼ cup basil white wine vinegar
3 tablespoons extra-virgin olive oil
2 tablespoons fresh basil, minced
2 tablespoon fresh parsley, minced
¼ teaspoon sweet paprika
   Salt and freshly ground black pepper to taste

In a large nonreactive bowl, combine the barley, green and red sweet peppers, and corn.

In a small nonreactive bowl, whisk together vinegar, olive oil, basil, parsley, paprika, salt, and pepper. Pour vinegar mixture over the barley mixture and toss until all ingredients are coated. Cover and refrigerate for several hours before serving to allow flavors to blend.

Sweet-and-Sour Lentils

Yield: 4 servings

2 cups vegetable stock or water
1 cup dry orange lentils
2 tablespoons canola oil
½ cup onion, chopped
1 clove garlic, minced
1 jalapeño pepper, cored, seeded, and minced
¼ cup hot pepper sherry vinegar
2 tablespoons honey
¼ teaspoon ground cloves
1 tablespoon fresh parsley, minced

Combine stock or water and lentils in a heavy saucepan and bring to a boil over medium-high heat. Reduce heat to low, cover saucepan, and cook until tender, or about 25 minutes.

In a large, heavy nonreactive skillet, warm oil over medium heat. Add onion, garlic, and jalapeño pepper and sauté until softened, or about 5 minutes, stirring occasionally. Stir in vinegar, honey, and cloves and cook for 1 minute. Stir in cooked lentils and parsley.

DILLED PASTA SALAD

Yield: 4 servings

- ½ pound dry angel hair pasta
- ¼ cup dill white wine vinegar
- 3 tablespoons extra-virgin olive oil
- 2 tablespoons red onion, minced
- 2 tablespoons fresh dill, minced
- 1 tablespoon fresh parsley, minced
- 1 tablespoon sweet red pepper, minced
  Salt and freshly ground black pepper to taste

Cook pasta until *al dente,* drain, rinse with cold water, and drain thoroughly. Place in a large shallow nonreactive bowl. Mix with 1 tablespoon olive oil. In a small nonreactive bowl, whisk together vinegar, remaining olive oil, onion, dill, parsley, sweet pepper, salt, and black pepper. Pour over pasta and toss to coat. Cover and chill for several hours before serving to allow flavors to blend.

ASPARAGUS-PECAN PASTA SALAD

Yield: 4 servings

- 8 ounces dry fettuccine
- 1 pound asparagus, trimmed and cut into 1-inch pieces
- 1 cup cherry tomatoes, halved
- ½ cup black imported olives, pitted and chopped
- ½ cup pecans, chopped and toasted
- 1½ cups fresh basil leaves
- ½ cup extra-virgin olive oil
- ¼ cup Parmesan cheese, freshly grated
- ¼ cup raw pecans, chopped
- ¼ cup basil red wine vinegar
- 1 clove garlic
  Salt and freshly ground black pepper to taste

Cook pasta until *al dente,* drain, rinse with cold water, and drain thoroughly. Place in a large shallow bowl. Mix with 1 tablespoon olive oil.

Bring salted water to a boil in a saucepan. Add asparagus and cook for 3 minutes. Drain, rinse with cold water, and drain again. Stir asparagus, tomatoes, olives, and toasted pecans into the pasta. In a blender or food processor, combine basil, remaining olive oil, Parmesan cheese, raw pecans, vinegar, garlic, salt, and pepper, and process until smooth. Pour dressing over pasta mixture and toss until all ingredients are coated. Cover and refrigerate for several hours.

VEGETABLES

Sautéed Green Peppers

Yield: 2 cups

2 sweet green peppers, cored, seeded, and sliced
⅔ cup extra-virgin olive oil
¼ cup coriander or garlic red wine vinegar
4 cloves garlic
¼ teaspoon salt
¼ teaspoon sweet paprika
¼ teaspoon ground coriander seeds

Combine all ingredients in a heavy nonreactive saucepan. Cook over low heat until the peppers are tender, or about 20 minutes. Place in a covered nonreactive bowl and refrigerate for several hours before serving.

Variation. Substitute yellow or red sweet peppers for the green.

Spicy Steamed Eggplant

Yield: 4 servings

1¼ pounds baby eggplant, cut into 1-inch pieces
3 tablespoons soy sauce
2 tablespoons sesame oil
2 tablespoons chive or garlic chive rice vinegar
2 tablespoons chives or garlic chives, minced
1 teaspoon honey
½ teaspoon hot red pepper sauce
1 clove garlic, minced

Steam the eggplant for 20 minutes, or until tender. Combine the remaining ingredients in a nonreactive bowl. Place the cooked eggplant in a nonreactive bowl and pour the sauce over it, tossing to coat. Serve immediately, at room temperature, or chilled.

73

Horseradish Beets

Yield: 4 servings

- 1 pound whole baby beets, cooked
- ⅔ cup beet cooking liquid or water
- 2 tablespoons honey
- 2 tablespoons horseradish red wine vinegar
- 1 tablespoon cornstarch
- 2 tablespoons horseradish, grated (fresh or preserved in vinegar)
- 1 tablespoon butter
- Salt and freshly ground black pepper to taste

In a nonreactive saucepan, combine beet cooking liquid or water and honey. Bring to a boil over medium heat.

In a small nonreactive bowl, combine vinegar and cornstarch and mix until smooth. Stir into hot liquid, and heat, stirring constantly, for several minutes, or until thickened. Add the beets, stirring to coat well, and heat through. Stir in the horseradish and butter and heat until butter is melted. Season with salt and pepper.

Marinated Fresh Cucumbers

Yield: 4 cups

- 6 medium cucumbers, peeled, seeded, and cut lengthwise into 12 strips
- 1½ tablespoons salt
- Six 4-inch dill sprigs
- 2 shallots, thinly sliced
- 1 clove garlic, thinly sliced
- 12 whole black peppercorns
- 2 bay leaves
- 1 small hot red fresh or dried pepper
- 1 tablespoon mustard seeds
- 1 teaspoon dill seeds
- ½ teaspoon mixed pickling spices
- 1½ cup water
- ½ cup dill white wine vinegar

In a large nonreactive bowl, toss the cucumber strips with the salt, cover, and let stand at room temperature for 24 hours. Drain the cucumber strips, rinse with cold water, and pat dry. Place the cucumber strips with the dill sprigs, shallots, garlic, peppercorns, bay leaves, hot pepper, mustard and dill seeds, and pickling spices in a sterilized quart canning jar. Combine the water and vinegar and pour over cucumber mixture. Cover tightly and refrigerate. Wait several days to allow flavors to blend before serving.

Mediterranean Vegetables

Yield: 6 servings

- 1 cup black imported olives, pitted and chopped
- 1 cup artichoke hearts, cooked
- 1 cup broccoli, cooked
- ½ pound mushrooms, sliced
- ½ cup sweet red peppers, roasted, peeled, cored, seeded, and diced
- ½ cup green onion, thinly sliced
- ⅓ cup basil-garlic red wine vinegar
- ⅓ cup extra-virgin olive oil
- 1 clove garlic, minced
- ½ teaspoon salt
- ½ teaspoon honey
- 1 teaspoon fresh basil, minced
- 1 teaspoon fresh marjoram, minced

Combine olives, artichoke hearts, broccoli, mushrooms, peppers, and onion in a nonreactive serving bowl.

In a small nonreactive bowl, whisk together the vinegar, oil, garlic, salt, honey, basil, and marjoram. Pour this mixture over the vegetables and stir to coat. Refrigerate for several hours to allow flavors to blend. Serve chilled or at room temperature.

Glazed Red Onions

Yield: 4 servings

- 2 tablespoons extra-virgin olive oil
- 1 large red onion, thinly sliced
- 1 tablespoon raisins
- 3 tablespoons thyme red wine or sherry vinegar
- 2 teaspoons fresh thyme, minced
- ½ teaspoon honey
  Salt and freshly ground black pepper to taste

Warm oil in a heavy nonreactive skillet over medium heat. Add onion and sauté, stirring often, until softened, or about 5 minutes. Add remaining ingredients and stir well. Cook until glaze is thickened, or about 4 minutes. Season with salt and pepper. Serve warm or at room temperature.

Zucchini with Sour Cream and Thyme

Yield: 4 servings

- 3 tablespoons canola oil
- 1 pound zucchini, shredded
- 2 tablespoons thyme red wine vinegar
- 2 teaspoons fresh thyme, minced
- ½ cup low-fat or nonfat sour cream
  Salt and freshly ground black pepper to taste

In a heavy nonreactive skillet, warm oil over medium heat. Add the squash and sauté until golden, or about 4 minutes. Remove and set aside. Add the vinegar to the pan, scraping up any bits on the bottom. Cook until reduced to a teaspoon. Add thyme and sour cream, mixing well. Return squash to skillet and stir to coat. Heat through and season with salt and pepper.

Dilled Potatoes

Yield: 4 servings

- ¼ cup canola oil
- 1 pound small red new potatoes, cut in half
- 3 tablespoons dill white wine or rice vinegar
- 3 tablespoons fresh dill, minced
  Salt and freshly ground black pepper to taste

In a heavy nonreactive skillet, warm the oil over medium heat. Add the potatoes and sauté, stirring frequently, until lightly browned and tender, or about 15 minutes. Add vinegar and cook for another 3 minutes. Sprinkle with dill and season with salt and pepper.

Herbed Lima Beans

Yield: 4 servings

- 1 tablespoon canola oil
- ½ cup onion, diced
- 1 clove garlic, minced
- 1 pound fresh baby lima beans, shelled
- 1 cup water
- ¼ cup mixed-herb white wine or rice vinegar
- 3 tablespoons fresh parsley, minced
- 1 tablespoon fresh thyme, minced
- 1 tablespoon fresh marjoram, minced
- Salt and freshly ground black pepper to taste

In a nonreactive saucepan, warm the oil over medium heat. Add the onion and garlic and sauté, stirring occasionally, until soft, or about 5 minutes. Add the lima beans, water, vinegar, parsley, thyme, and marjoram. Cook until the beans are tender, or about 5 to 10 minutes. Season to taste.

Carrots with Tomatoes and Fennel

Yield: 4 servings

- 2 tablespoons butter
- ½ cup onion, finely chopped
- 1 clove garlic, minced
- 2 cups carrots, peeled and thinly sliced
- ½ cup tomato, peeled, seeded, and diced
- 3 tablespoons fennel sherry vinegar
- 3 tablespoons fresh fennel, minced
- 2 tablespoons water
- Salt and freshly ground black pepper to taste

In a nonreactive saucepan, melt butter over medium heat. Add onion and garlic. Stirring, sauté until translucent, or about 3 minutes. Add carrots, tomato, vinegar, fennel, and water. Cover, reduce heat to low, and simmer just until carrots are tender, or about 6 to 10 minutes. Season with salt and pepper.

Minted Carrots

Yield: 4 servings

  1 pound baby carrots
1½ cups water
 ½ cup unsweetened mint vinegar
  1 tablespoon fresh spearmint, minced
 ½ teaspoon fresh thyme, minced
     Salt and freshly ground black pepper to taste

Peel carrots, if necessary, and place in nonreactive saucepan. Add water, vinegar, mint, and thyme to pan. Bring to a boil over medium heat and cook about 10 minutes, or until carrots are tender. Season with salt and pepper. Serve carrots warm or chilled.

Carrots Glazed with Ginger and Lemon Thyme

Yield: 4 servings

  1 pound carrots, cut into 2-inch matchsticks
  4 tablespoons butter
  2 tablespoons shallot, minced
  2 tablespoons candied ginger, minced
  2 tablespoons lemon thyme white wine or rice vinegar
  1 tablespoon fresh lemon thyme, minced
     Salt and freshly ground black pepper, to taste

In a saucepan, combine carrots with water to cover. Bring to a boil over medium heat, reduce heat to low, cover, and poach until tender, or about 5 minutes. Drain, rinse with cold running water, and drain again. Set aside.

In a heavy nonreactive skillet, melt butter over medium heat. Add shallot and ginger and sauté until softened, or about 3 minutes, stirring occasionally. Add vinegar, lemon thyme, and carrots, stirring to coat, and heat through for 2 to 3 minutes. Season with salt and pepper.

Leeks Glazed with Sage and Maple

Yield: 4 servings

- 8 medium leeks
- 2 tablespoons olive oil
- 1 tablespoon butter
- 2 cloves garlic, minced
- 2 tablespoons water
- 3 tablespoons sage sherry vinegar
- 2 teaspoons maple syrup
- 2 teaspoons fresh sage, minced
- 1 teaspoon Dijon mustard

Trim the leeks, removing all but ½ inch of the green tops. Wash well and dry. Cut leeks into 1-inch slices.

In a large heavy nonreactive skillet, warm the oil and butter over medium heat. Add garlic and sauté until softened. Add leeks, stirring to coat surfaces with the oil and butter. Arrange in a single layer in the skillet. Add water. Cover and cook on very low heat for 20 minutes, or until tender. Check occasionally to make sure leeks are not sticking.

In a nonreactive bowl, combine vinegar, maple syrup, sage, and mustard. Pour over the tender leeks, gently stirring to coat surface.

Kale with Tomatoes

Yield: 4 servings

- 1½ pounds kale, stems removed
- 1 tablespoon olive oil
- 1 clove garlic, minced
- ½ cup green onions, thinly sliced
- 2 medium tomatoes, peeled, seeded, and diced
- 2 tablespoons fresh tarragon, minced
- 2 tablespoons tarragon white wine vinegar
- ¼ teaspoon hot red pepper flakes or sauce
  Salt and freshly ground black pepper to taste

Wash the kale thoroughly, shake off excess water, and coarsely chop. In a large heavy nonreactive skillet, warm the olive oil over medium heat. Add the garlic and onion and sauté for 1 minute, stirring occasionally. Add the kale, stirring to coat the leaves. Cover the pan, and cook until the kale is wilted and tender, or about 3 minutes. Add tomatoes, tarragon, vinegar, hot pepper, salt, and pepper. Heat through for 3 minutes, stirring occasionally.

Roasted Garlic

Serve as an accompaniment to roasted or grilled meats, as a topping for baked or mashed potatoes, or as a spread for toasted French bread slices.

Yield: 2 to 4 servings

- 2 whole garlic heads
- 2 tablespoons extra-virgin olive oil
- 2 tablespoons rosemary sherry vinegar
- 1 tablespoon fresh rosemary, minced

Preheat oven to 300°F. Slice the tops from the heads of garlic and remove most of the papery outer skin, but do not peel or separate into cloves. Place in a small ovenproof nonreactive dish. Pour the olive oil and vinegar over the tops of the garlic and add the rosemary. Cover with a lid or aluminum foil. Bake until very tender, or about 1 hour.

Dilled Potato Salad

Yield: 4 servings

- 1 pound small new potatoes, cooked and sliced
- ½ cup peas, cooked
- ¼ cup celery, thinly sliced
- ¼ cup green onion, thinly sliced
- ¼ cup reduced-calorie mayonnaise
- ¼ cup plain nonfat yogurt
- 3 tablespoons fresh dill, minced
- 2 tablespoons dill white wine vinegar
- 2 teaspoons Dijon mustard
- ½ teaspoon sugar
- 1 clove garlic, minced
  Salt and freshly ground black pepper

In a large nonreactive bowl, combine potatoes, peas, celery, and green onion. In a small bowl, combine remaining ingredients. Pour over the potato mixture and toss until all ingredients are coated. Cover and refrigerate for several hours before serving to allow flavors to blend.

Variations. Substitute another flavored vinegar with corresponding herbs for the dill. Substitute summer squash or lightly steamed carrots for the peas. Pitted imported black olives are also a nice addition to potato salad.

Spiced Red Cabbage with Apples and Onions

Yield: 4 servings

- 2 tablespoons canola oil
- 1 medium red onion, thinly sliced
- 2 apples, cored and diced
- 2 pounds red cabbage, finely shredded
- ½ cup dry red wine
- ½ cup vegetable stock or water
- ¼ cup mixed-spice red wine vinegar
- 2 tablespoons packed light brown sugar or one tablespoon honey
- 4 whole cloves
  One 3-inch cinnamon stick
  Salt and freshly ground black pepper to taste

Warm oil in a large, heavy nonreactive saucepan over medium heat. Add onion and apples and sauté until golden, or about 6 minutes, stirring occasionally. Add remaining ingredients and stir to combine. Reduce heat to low, cover, and cook until the cabbage is tender, or about 25 minutes. Remove cinnamon stick and whole cloves before serving.

Cabbage and Jalapeño Slaw

Yield: 4 servings

- 4 cups cabbage, finely shredded
- 1½ cups sweet red pepper, cored, seeded, and diced
- ½ cup green onion, thinly sliced
- 1 fresh jalapeño pepper, cored, seeded, and minced
- 1 clove garlic, minced
- 1 tablespoon fresh marjoram, minced
- ½ cup extra-virgin olive oil
- 3 tablespoons marjoram white wine vinegar
- 1 tablespoon water or dry white wine
- ½ teaspoon ground cumin seeds
- ½ teaspoon sugar
  Salt and freshly ground black pepper to taste

In large nonreactive bowl, toss together cabbage, red pepper, green onion, jalapeño pepper, garlic, and marjoram. In small nonreactive bowl, whisk olive oil, vinegar, water or wine, cumin, sugar, salt, and pepper. Pour dressing over slaw. Toss lightly to mix well. Cover; refrigerate several hours.

Marinated Mushrooms

Yield: 4 servings

- 4 cups water
- 1 teaspoon salt
- 1 pound small white mushrooms, trimmed and rinsed
- ½ cup mixed-herb sherry vinegar
- ¼ cup onion, minced
- 2 cloves garlic, minced
- 1 bay leaf
- 1 teaspoon fresh thyme, minced
- ½ teaspoon fennel seeds
- ½ teaspoon hot red pepper flakes
- ¼ cup extra-virgin olive oil
- 1 teaspoon fresh parsley, minced

Combine water and salt in a heavy saucepan and bring to a boil over medium heat. Add mushrooms and boil for 2 minutes. Drain, reserving ½ cup of the liquid.

In a heavy nonreactive saucepan combine the reserved liquid, vinegar, onion, garlic, bay leaf, thyme, fennel seeds, and pepper flakes and simmer for 5 minutes. Remove from heat and stir in the oil and parsley. Place the mushrooms in a nonreactive bowl or jar and pour the vinegar mixture over them. Cover and refrigerate for 24 hours before serving.

Tomato-and-Bread Salad

Yield: 4 servings

- 4 cups plum tomatoes, peeled, seeded, and diced
- 1½ cups cucumber, peeled, seeded, and diced
- ½ cup green onion, thinly sliced
- ¼ cup fresh basil, minced
- ¼ cup fresh parsley, minced
- 1 tablespoon fresh thyme, minced
- 2 cloves garlic, minced
- ¼ cup extra-virgin olive oil
- ¼ cup basil red wine vinegar
- 2½ cups ½-inch stale Italian bread cubes, lightly toasted

In a large nonreactive bowl, combine all ingredients except bread cubes. Cover and refrigerate for at least 1 hour. Just before serving, add bread cubes and toss mixture well.

SALAD DRESSINGS

The composition of an oil-and-vinegar dressing, or vinaigrette, is essentially a vinegar and an oil, such as olive or canola, plus salt, pepper, various herbs, and other seasonings. There are no hard-and-fast rules, although traditionally there is more oil than vinegar. For a long time the favored proportions were four parts oil to one part vinegar. These proportions have narrowed somewhat with the desire to limit fat intake. The proportions most commonly suggested now are three to one or two to one. High-quality, milder-flavored vinegars are essential. Use the best oil possible, preferably an extra-virgin olive oil or an organically grown and expeller-processed canola, safflower, or untoasted sesame oil. Experiment with the more unusual oils, such as walnut, hazlenut, or avocado.

I seldom follow a dressing recipe to the letter. I'm more likely to be influenced by what is in the garden, pantry, or refrigerator. I encourage you to experiment with both proportions and ingredients as well. Sweet herbs and fruit vinegars yield dressings ideal for fruit salads. The addition of heavy cream, sour cream, mayonnaise, plain yogurt, buttermilk, avocado, or silken tofu makes a creamy dressing. Besides the basic ingredients of oil, vinegar, and herbs, try the optional ingredients listed on page 84.

The preparation of an oil-and-vinegar dressing can be as simple as combining the ingredients in a jar, securing the lid, and shaking, or whisking the ingredients together in a small nonreactive bowl. For a thicker, more emulsified dressing, combine all ingredients except oil in a bowl or blender, then add the oil in a very slow stream, simultaneously whisking the mixture or running the blender.

Be willing to use these flavorsome mixtures in a wide variety of ways. Obviously, they can serve as a dressing for a simple salad of greens fresh from the garden. Used as a marinade for steamed, grilled, or sautéed vegetables, they enrich flavor whether the dishes are served warm, at room temperature, or chilled. Marinating poultry, beef, lamb, pork, fish, or tofu before and during baking, roasting, or grilling yields a tender, well-seasoned main course.

Basic Ingredients for Vinaigrette

Extra-virgin olive, canola, safflower, or nut oil

Flavored vinegar

Minced fresh herbs

Whole or ground herb seeds and spices

Salt and freshly ground black pepper

Additions or Substitutions

Dry or prepared mustard (prepared mustards give a creamier texture)

Sugar, honey, barley malt, or maple syrup

Minced fresh garlic cloves

Roasted garlic or shallots

Minced fresh green onion, red onion, white onion, sweet onion, or shallot

Minced fresh sweet red, green, purple, yellow, or orange pepper

Minced fresh hot red or green pepper

Minced fresh celery

Minced olives

Chopped nuts

Minced citrus zest

Hot pepper sauce or ground cayenne pepper

Soy sauce

Worcestershire sauce

Dry white or red wine, vermouth, port, sherry, or madeira

Vegetable or chicken stock

Freshly grated Parmesan or Romano cheese

Crumbled blue cheese, feta cheese, or fresh goat cheese

Ketchup

Chili sauce

Chutney

Minced anchovy fillets

Chopped hard-boiled eggs

Capers

Minced pickled beets

Minced sour or sweet pickles

Relish

Tomato Dressing

Serve over baked or grilled eggplant cut into chunks, roasted sweet red pepper slices, steamed vegetables, or any green salad.

Yield: 1¼ cups

- ⅔ cup tomato juice
- ¼ cup extra-virgin olive oil
- ¼ cup basil sherry vinegar
- 2 tablespoons sun-dried tomatoes, minced
- 2 tablespoons fresh basil, minced
- 1 tablespoon fresh lemon juice
- Salt and freshly ground black pepper to taste

Whisk all ingredients together in a nonreactive bowl. Cover and refrigerate for 1 hour before useing to allow flavors to blend. Store in a tightly covered jar in the refrigerator.

Creamy Low-Calorie Tomato Dressing

Yield: 1½ cups

- ¾ cup tomato juice
- ½ cup low-fat or nonfat ricotta cheese
- ¼ cup tarragon white wine vinegar
- 1 large egg, hard-boiled and peeled
- 1 tablespoon soy sauce
- 1 tablespoon fresh tarragon, minced
- Freshly ground black pepper to taste

Combine all ingredients in a blender and process until smooth. Cover and refrigerate for 1 hour before serving to allow flavors to blend. Store in a tightly covered jar in the refrigerator.

Variation. Substitute other flavored vinegars and herbs for the tarragon.

Ricotta Low-Calorie Dressing

Yield: ¾ cup

- ½ cup low-fat or nonfat ricotta cheese
- ¼ cup tarragon white wine vinegar
- 1 tablespoon water, white wine, cream, buttermilk, or skim milk
- 1 teaspoon Dijon mustard
- 1 teaspoon capers
- 1 teaspoon fresh tarragon, minced
- 1 teaspoon fresh garlic chives, minced
- 1 oil-packed anchovy filet, drained and minced
- ½ teaspoon hot red pepper sauce

Combine all ingredients in a nonreactive bowl or blender until smooth. Cover and chill for several hours before using to allow flavors to blend. Store in a tightly covered jar in the refrigerator.

Creamy Dressing

Great for tossed green salads, use different flavored vinegars and herbs for this dressing. Double the amount of mayonnaise or use a 3-ounce package of low-fat cream cheese to turn this dressing into a dip.

Yield: 1 cup

- ⅔ cup plain nonfat yogurt or low-fat or nonfat sour cream
- ⅓ cup reduced-calorie mayonnaise
- 2 tablespoons flavored vinegar
- 2 tablespoons fresh herbs, minced, 1 tablespoon herb seeds, or 1 tablespoon fresh ginger or horseradish, minced
- 1 teaspoon Dijon mustard
- ¼ teaspoon freshly ground black pepper or hot red pepper sauce

Whisk all ingredients together in a nonreactive bowl. Let sit an hour before using to allow flavors to blend. Store in a tightly covered jar in the refrigerator.

Variations. Vary this dressing by reversing the proportions of yogurt or sour cream with the mayonnaise or by using equal proportions. A sweeter dressing is made by adding 1 tablespoon of honey. To make Green Goddess Dressing, use more mayonnaise than yogurt or sour cream and add 2 drained minced anchovy fillets, 1 minced clove garlic, and minced chives and parsley for the herbs. Or, use minced basil, tarragon, and chives, 1 minced clove garlic, and 1 tablespoon Worcestershire sauce.

DILL-BURNET CREAM DRESSING

Yield: ⅔ cup

- ½ cup low-fat or nonfat sour cream
- ¼ cup green onions, thinly sliced, or fresh chives, minced
- ¼ cup fresh burnet, minced
- 2 tablespoons burnet white wine vinegar
- 1 tablespoon fresh dill, minced, or ½ teaspoon dill seed

In a small nonreactive bowl, combine all ingredients. Cover and refrigerate for at least 1 hour before serving. Store in a tightly covered jar in the refrigerator.

CREAMY ROMANO DRESSING

Yield: 1¼ cups

- ½ cup extra-virgin olive oil
- ½ cup Romano cheese, freshly grated
- 1 clove garlic, minced or 1 tablespoon fresh garlic chives, minced
- ¼ cup buttermilk
- 3 tablespoons mixed -herb white wine vinegar
- 2 tablespoons mixed fresh herbs, minced
- 1 teaspoon honey
- Salt and freshly ground black pepper to taste

Combine all ingredients in a blender and process until smooth. For a more emulsified dressing, blend all ingredients except oil, then slowly drizzle in the oil with the blender running. Cover and chill for several hours before using to allow flavors to blend. Store, tightly covered, in the refrigerator.

CREAMY HERB DRESSING

Yield: 2 cups

- 1 cup extra-virgin olive oil
- ½ cup buttermilk
- ¼ cup fresh parsley, minced
- ¼ cup fresh basil, minced
- 3 tablespoons mixed-herb white wine vinegar
- 2 tablespoons water
- 2 tablespoons fresh thyme, minced
- 1 tablespoon fresh chives, minced
- 1 tablespoon honey
- 1 green onion, thinly sliced
- 1 teaspoon Dijon mustard

Combine all ingredients in a blender and process until smooth. For a more emulsified dressing, blend all ingredients except oil, then slowly drizzle in the oil with the blender running. Cover and chill for several hours before using to allow flavors to blend. Store, tightly covered, in the refrigerator.

CREAMY RASPBERRY DRESSING

Serve with bibb or butterhead lettuce sprinkled with fresh raspberries and toasted walnuts.

Yield: ⅔ cup

- ⅓ cup plain nonfat yogurt or low-fat or nonfat sour cream
- ¼ cup fresh raspberries
- 3 tablespoons raspberry vinegar
- 2 tablespoons reduced-calorie mayonnaise
- 1 tablespoon Dijon mustard
- 1 teaspoon sugar
  Freshly ground black pepper to taste

In a nonreactive bowl, whisk together all ingredients. Cover; chill for several hours before using to allow flavors to blend. Store, tightly covered, in the refrigerator.

Avocado Dressing

Yield: 1¼ cups

½ cup extra-virgin olive oil
¼ cup dill or tarragon white wine vinegar
1 avocado, peeled and pitted
¼ cup green onion, thinly sliced
1 tablespoon fresh dill, minced
1 tablespoon fresh lovage or celery leaves, minced
1 teaspoon fresh tarragon, minced
Salt and freshly ground black pepper to taste

Combine all ingredients in a blender and process until smooth. Cover and chill for several hours before using to allow flavors to blend. Store, tightly covered, in the refrigerator.

The Cook's Garden Ginger Dressing

Yield: 1 cup

½ cup extra-virgin olive oil
¼ cup chopped crystallized ginger
¼ cup ginger rice vinegar
2 tablespoons soy sauce
2 tablespoons honey
2 tablespoons fresh lemon juice
1 tablespoon Dijon mustard
1 teaspoon untoasted sesame oil
1 small hot red pepper

In a small heavy nonreactive saucepan, combine all ingredients. Bring to a boil over medium heat, reduce heat to low, and simmer for 3 minutes. Remove hot pepper. Pour over oriental greens while still hot.

HONEY-FLOWER DRESSING

Yield: 1¼ cups

- ¾ cup canola oil
- ¼ cup honey, warmed
- ¼ cup flower vinegar
- 2 tablespoons flower petals, such as roses, carnations, or violets, minced
- 1 teaspoon Dijon mustard
- 1 teaspoon sweet paprika
- 1 teaspoon poppy seeds
- Salt and freshly ground black pepper to taste

Combine all ingredients in a blender or food processor and process until smooth. Cover and chill for several hours before using to allow flavors to blend. Store in a tightly covered jar in the refrigerator.

CITRUS DRESSING

Yield: 1 cup

- ½ cup canola or safflower oil
- ¼ cup lime or orange white wine or rice vinegar
- 3 tablespoons lime or orange juice
- 2 tablespoons shallots, minced
- 2 tablespoons fresh parsley, minced
- 1 tablespoon fresh ginger, minced
- 1 teaspoon soy or Worcestershire sauce
- 1 teaspoon fresh lime or orange zest
- 1 teaspoon sugar
- ½ teaspoon hot red pepper sauce
- Salt and freshly ground black pepper to taste

Combine all ingredients in a nonreactive bowl, jar, or blender and mix until well blended. Cover and chill for several hours before using to allow flavors to blend. Store, tightly covered, in the refrigerator.

Asian Dressing

Yield: 1 cup

- ½ cup untoasted sesame oil
- ¼ cup ginger sherry vinegar
- ¼ cup green onions, thinly sliced
- ¼ cup fresh cilantro, minced
- 2 tablespoons tahini (optional)
- 1 tablespoon fresh ginger, minced
- 1 tablespoon soy sauce
- 1 teaspoon hot red pepper sauce
- 1 teaspoon honey
- 1 teaspoon ground cumin
- 1 clove garlic, minced

Combine all ingredients in a nonreactive bowl or blender until smooth. Cover and chill for several hours before using to allow flavors to blend. Store, tightly covered, in the refrigerator.

Middle Eastern Spice Dressing

Yield: ⅔ cup

- ¼ cup extra-virgin olive, canola, or safflower oil
- 2 tablespoons shallots or mild onion, minced
- 1 clove garlic, minced
- 2 tablespoons fresh spearmint, minced
- 2 tablespoons pine nuts or pistachios, chopped
- 1 tablespoon dried currants
- ¼ teaspoon ground cinnamon
- ¼ teaspoon ground allspice
- ¼ cup mixed-spice red wine vinegar
- 2 tablespoons low-fat or nonfat sour cream

Warm oil in a medium-size heavy nonreactive skillet over medium heat. Add shallots and garlic and sauté until softened, or about 2 to 3 minutes, stirring occasionally. Add mint, currants, nuts, cinnamon, and allspice, stirring to combine. Continuing to stir, sauté for 3 minutes. Remove from heat and stir in vinegar, then sour cream. Immediately pour over greens.

GREEN DRESSING

Yield: 1¼ cups

  1 cup fresh chard or sorrel
  ¾ cup fresh parsley
  ¼ cup fresh basil
  ½ cup extra-virgin olive oil
  ¼ cup mixed-spice sherry vinegar
  ½ teaspoon curry powder
  1 clove garlic, minced
    Salt and freshly ground black pepper to taste

Combine all ingredients in a blender and process until smooth. Cover and chill for several hours before using to allow flavors to blend. Store, tightly covered, in the refrigerator.

HOT-AND-SOUR DRESSING

Yield: 1 cup

  ½ cup vegetable stock or unsweetened coconut milk
  ¼ cup ginger rice vinegar
  2 tablespoons untoasted sesame oil
  2 tablespoons creamy peanut butter or tahini
  1 tablespoon dry white wine
  1 tablespoon soy sauce
  2 teaspoons sesame seeds, toasted
  1 teaspoon fresh ginger, minced
  1 clove garlic, minced
  ½ teaspoon hot red pepper sauce

Combine all ingredients in a nonreactive bowl, jar, or blender and mix until well blended. Cover and chill for several hours before using to allow flavors to blend. Store, tightly covered, in the refrigerator.

Boiled Dressing

Yield: 1½ cups

   1 tablespoon sugar
1½ teaspoons cornstarch
   1 teaspoon dry English mustard
   1 teaspoon salt
   ¼ teaspoon ground cayenne pepper
   ½ cup mixed-herb white wine or cider vinegar
   1 large whole egg and 1 large egg yolk, both lightly beaten
   1 cup milk or half-and-half
   ¼ cup fresh herbs, minced

In the top of a nonreactive double boiler over simmering water, combine sugar, cornstarch, mustard, salt, and cayenne. Slowly stir in vinegar, egg and egg yolk until well blended. Whisk in milk or half-and-half. Whisking constantly, cook the mixture until thickened. If desired, strain through a fine sieve into a bowl. Let the dressing cool to room temperature and stir in herbs. Store in a tightly covered jar in the refrigerator.

Sesame Dressing

Yield: 1½ cups

   1 cup low-fat or nonfat ricotta cheese
   ¼ cup untoasted sesame oil
   ¼ cup ginger or cilantro rice vinegar
   2 tablespoons fresh cilantro, minced
   2 tablespoons fresh parsley, minced
   2 tablespoons sesame seeds, toasted
   1 tablespoon fresh ginger, minced
   ½ teaspoon ground cayenne pepper
   1 clove garlic, minced

Combine all ingredients in a blender or food processor and process until smooth. Cover and chill for several hours before using to allow flavors to blend. Store in a tightly covered jar in the refrigerator.

Fruit Dressing

Use this dressing for fruit salads. Vary the juice, vinegar, and herbs used.

Yield: ½ cup

- ¼ cup fruit juice
- 2 tablespoons fruit vinegar
- 2 tablespoons canola or safflower oil
- 1 tablespoon fresh anise hyssop, mint, sweet cicely, lavender, or angelica, minced
- 1 teaspoon honey

Combine all ingredients in a nonreactive jar or bowl. Cover and chill for several hours before using to allow flavors to blend. Store in a tightly covered jar in the refrigerator.

Melon-Mint Dressing

Yield: 1 cup

- ½ cup low-fat or nonfat sour cream or vanilla nonfat yogurt
- ¼ cup mint white wine vinegar
- 3 tablespoons fresh spearmint, minced
- 1 cup cantaloupe, chopped

Combine all ingredients in a blender or food processor and process until smooth. Cover and chill for several hours before using to allow flavors to blend. Store in a tightly covered jar in the refrigerator.

Hot Mushroom Dressing

Yield: 1 cup

- ¼ cup extra-virgin olive oil
- 8 ounces mushrooms, thinly sliced
- ¼ cup green onion, thinly sliced
- ¼ cup mixed-herb white wine or rice vinegar
- 2 tablespoons fresh herbs, minced
- ½ teaspoon honey
  Salt and freshly ground black pepper to taste

Warm oil in a medium-size heavy nonreactive skillet over medium heat. Add mushrooms and green onions and sauté until softened, or about 3 to 5 minutes, stirring occasionally. Add vinegar, herbs, sugar, salt, and pepper, stirring to combine. Immediately pour over greens, such as spinach.

MARINADES

 e now cook and eat grilled food almost year-round. For the best flavor, foods are often either steeped in a seasoned liquid — marinated — prior to grilling, or they are basted during cooking. Basting sauces are also usually served with the food. In many cases, foods are both marinated and basted, and the distinctions between the two can be somewhat nebulous.

At its most basic, a marinade contains only oil and seasonings. This combination simply moistens the surface of the food to prevent evaporation of the natural juices during cooking, spreads the flavor of the seasonings over the surface, and prevents the surface from sticking to the grill. With the addition of an acidic liquid, such as vinegar, fruit juice, wine, or soured milk products, the marinade also tenderizes and causes the seasonings to penetrate.

Foods are usually marinated for several hours or overnight and kept, covered, in the refrigerator until 30 minutes before grilling. Because of the acidity, the food is marinated in a nonreactive dish, preferably glass or ceramic. If foods are not totally submerged, they should be turned several times during the marinating.

Almost any salad dressing can be used as a marinade, but there are also mixtures that are specifically for marinating. Experiment with different kinds of oils, vinegars, and seasonings, as you do with salad dressings. The best soy sauces are available at health food stores and are called *tamari* or *shoyu*.

Basting sauces containing sugar, honey, molasses, or fruit juice should be applied only after the food is partially cooked so that they will not burn before the food is done. For basting, try the Easy Plum Sauce (page 102) and Barbecue Sauce (page 110) as well as the chutneys or ketchups.

MEXICAN MARINADE

Use with chicken, pork, or beef.

Yield: 1¾ cups

- ¾   cup onion, minced
- ¾   cup garlic cider vinegar
- ⅓   cup fresh hot green pepper, cored, seeded, and minced
- 3   tablespoons fresh cilantro, minced
- 2   cloves garlic, minced
- 1   teaspoon salt

Combine all ingredients in a glass or ceramic dish.

COFFEE-MOLASSES MARINADE

Use with pork spareribs or chicken.

Yield: 2¼ cups

- 1   cup strong coffee
- ½   cup garlic red wine vinegar
- ¼   cup unsulfured molasses
- ¼   cup Dijon mustard
- 1   tablespoon Worcestershire sauce

In a small heavy nonreactive saucepan, combine all ingredients and bring to a boil over medium heat. Reduce heat to low and simmer for 2 minutes. Cool before transfering to a glass or ceramic dish.

MELON-CURRY MARINADE

Use with chicken or pork.

Yield: 1 cup

- 1   cup cantaloupe, diced
- ⅔   cup orange white wine vinegar
- ¼   cup canola or safflower oil
- 1   tablespoon curry powder
- 1   teaspoon salt

Combine all ingredients in a blender and process until smooth. Transfer to a glass or ceramic dish.

Red Wine Marinade

Use with beef or lamb.

Yield: 2 cups

- ¼ cup olive oil
- 1 cup onion, minced
- 2 cloves garlic, minced
- ½ cup garlic red wine vinegar
- ¾ cup dry red wine
- ½ cup water
- ¼ cup tomato paste
- 1 tablespoon fresh rosemary, minced
- 1 bay leaf

In a heavy nonreactive skillet, warm the oil over medium heat; add onion and garlic. Reduce heat to low and cook until softened (about 5 minutes). Stir in the vinegar and cook until reduced by half. Add the wine, water, tomato paste, rosemary and bay leaf. Simmer for 5 minutes. Let cool and transfer to a glass or ceramic dish.

Soy Marinade

Yield: 1½ cups

- ½ cup soy sauce
- ½ cup canola or safflower oil
- ¼ cup ginger rice or sherry vinegar
- ¼ cup dry sherry
- ¼ cup honey
- ¼ cup green onion, thinly sliced
- 2 tablespoons tomato paste
- 1 tablespoon fresh ginger, minced
- 2 cloves garlic, minced
- 1 teaspoon hot red pepper sauce

Combine all ingredients in a heavy nonreactive saucepan and bring to a boil over medium heat. Reduce heat and simmer for 5 minutes. Cool and transfer to a glass or ceramic dish.

Mediterranean Marinade

Use with chicken or lamb.

Yield: 2 cups

   1 cup olive oil
   1 cup onion, minced
  ⅓ cup rosemary white wine vinegar
   1 tablespoon fresh rosemary, minced
   1 teaspoon fresh thyme, minced
   1 teaspoon fresh marjoram, minced
   2 cloves garlic, minced
  ¼ teaspoon freshly ground black pepper

Combine all ingredients in a glass or ceramic dish.

Parsley-Shallot Marinade

Use with salmon, halibut, or swordfish.

Yield: 1 cup

  ½ cup olive oil
  ¼ cup shallots, minced
   1 clove garlic, minced
  ¼ cup fresh parsley, minced
   3 tablespoons lemon thyme white wine vinegar
   2 tablespoons fresh lemon thyme, minced

In a heavy nonreactive skillet, warm the oil over medium heat and add the shallots and garlic. Reduce heat to low and cook until softened, or about 5 minutes. Add remaining ingredients and simmer for 2 minutes. Let cool and transfer to a glass or ceramic dish.

Apple-Sage Marinade

Use with pork.

Yield: 1¼ cups

  ⅔ cup apple juice
  ⅓ cup canola or safflower oil
  ¼ cup sage cider vinegar
   2 tablespoons fresh sage, minced
   1 teaspoon salt

Combine all ingredients in a glass or ceramic dish.

Herb-Spice Marinade

Use with chicken or seafood.

Yield: 1½ cups

- 1 cup olive oil
- ¼ cup mixed-herb white wine vinegar
- ¼ cup fresh lemon juice
- 1 tablespoon fresh cilantro, minced
- 1 tablespoooon fresh chives, minced
- 1 teaspoon ground cumin seeds
- 1 clove garlic, minced

Combine all ingredients in a glass or ceramic dish.

Ginger-Sherry Marinade

Use with chicken or pork.

Yield: ¾ cup

- ½ cup soy sauce
- ¼ cup ginger sherry vinegar
- 2 tablespoons olive oil
- 1 tablespoon fresh ginger, minced
- 1 tablespoon shallots, minced
- 1 clove garlic, minced
- ¼ teaspoon freshly ground black pepper

Combine all ingredients in a glass or ceramic dish.

Soy-Citrus Marinade

Use with salmon, halibut, or swordfish.

Yield: ⅔ cup

- ¼ cup soy sauce
- 3 tablespoons orange white wine vinegar
- 2 tablespoons canola or safflower oil
- 1 tablespoon tomato paste
- 1 tablespoon fresh orange zest
- 1 tablespoon fresh parsley, minced
- 1 tablespoon fresh lemon basil, minced
- 1 clove garlic, minced
- ¼ teaspoon freshly ground black pepper

Combine all ingredients in a glass or ceramic dish.

White Wine Marinade

Use with chicken or pork.

Yield: 1¼ cups

- ⅔ cup dry white wine or vermouth
- 3 tablespoons olive oil
- 3 tablespoons mixed-herb or mixed-spice white wine vinegar
- ¼ cup green onion, thinly sliced
- ¼ cup lovage or celery leaves, minced
- 1 teaspoon fresh thyme, minced
- 1 teaspoon bruised juniper berries (optional)
- 1 bay leaf
- 1 clove garlic, minced
- ¼ teaspoon freshly ground black pepper

Combine all ingredients in a glass or ceramic dish.

Variation. Substitute red wine and red wine vinegar for the white and use other herbs, as desired.

Mustard-Tarragon Marinade

Use with lamb, chicken, salmon, swordfish, or halibut.

Yield: 1½ cups

- 1 cup olive oil
- ¼ cup tarragon white wine or rice vinegar
- ¼ cup Dijon mustard
- 1 tablespoon fresh tarragon, minced
- 2 cloves garlic, minced

Process all ingredients in a blender until smooth. Pour into a glass or ceramic dish.

CHAPTER 12

SAUCES AND SALSAS

HORSERADISH-BEET SAUCE

Serve this classic combination with roast beef.

Yield: About 2 cups

- 1 cup horseradish, grated
  (fresh or preserved in vinegar)
- 1 cup beets, cooked, peeled, and grated
- ¼ cup mixed-spice, garlic, or chili red wine vinegar
- 1 teaspoon salt
- 1 teaspoon sugar

Combine all ingredients in a nonreactive bowl. Taste and add more vinegar, if desired. Put mixture in a jar, cap it and refrigerate for at least several hours before using.

GINGER SAUCE

Serve with glazed chicken wings, sushi, steamed vegetables, or stir-fried dishes.

Yield: ¾ cup

- 1 small sweet onion, chopped
- ½ cup soy sauce
- ¼ cup ginger rice vinegar
- 1 tablespoon fresh cilantro
- 1 teaspoon honey
- 4 quarter-size slices fresh ginger

Combine all ingredients in a blender until smooth. Put mixture in a nonreactive jar, cap, and refrigerate for at least several hours before using.

Easy Plum Sauce

Yield: 1½ cups

>   12-ounce jar plum jam
> 2 teaspoons onion, minced
> 2 tablespoons ginger rice vinegar
> 1 tablespoon fresh ginger, minced
> ¼ teaspoon dry English mustard
> ¼ teaspoon hot red pepper sauce
> ⅛ teaspoon ground cinnamon
> ⅛ teaspoon ground nutmeg
> ⅛ teaspoon ground allspice
> ⅛ teaspoon ground cloves

Combine all ingredients in a heavy, nonreactive saucepan. Cook over low heat, stirring frequently, until jam is melted. Continue cooking and stirring for 5 minutes. Store in the refrigerator.

Mint Sauce

Serve with lamb, grilled seafood, or mixed with mayonnaise for salads.

Yield: 1 cup

> 1 cup mint white wine or rice vinegar
> 3 tablespoons honey
> ½ cup fresh spearmint, minced

Combine all ingredients in a nonreactive saucepan and bring just to a boil over medium heat. Remove from heat, pour into a bowl, cover, and chill.

Variations. Make with other fresh herbs, such as tarragon, chervil, lemon balm, lemon basil, or anise hyssop.

Adobo Sauce (Caribbean Garlic Sauce)

Use as an accompaniment or marinade for steaks, chickens, or pork.

Yield: ½ cup

- 6 cloves garlic
- 1 teaspoon fresh oregano
- 1 teaspoon fresh marjoram
- 2 tablespoons extra-virgin olive oil
- ½ cup oregano or marjoram white wine vinegar

Combine all ingredients in a blender until smooth. Put mixture in a jar, cap, and refrigerate for several hours before using.

White Butter Sauce

Using cream in this classic sauce allows it to be held longer without separating. Herbs to consider using include tarragon, parsley, chives, basil, chervil, cilantro, dill, fennel, basil, lemon basil, lemon balm, lemon thyme, thyme, sorrel, or marjoram.

Use with poached chicken, delicate fish, or vegetables.

Yield: ⅔ cup

- 2 tablespoons shallot, minced
- ½ cup herb-flavored white wine vinegar, matching the vinegar to the herb used
- 2 tablespoons heavy cream
- 1 stick (½ cup) cold butter, cut into 16 pieces
- 1 tablespoon fresh herbs, minced
- ¼ teaspoon salt
- ⅛ teaspoon freshly ground white pepper

In a small, heavy nonreactive saucepan, combine shallots and vinegar and cook over medium-high heat until reduced to about 2 tablespoons. Whisk in cream and reduce heat to low. Simmer until mixture is reduced to about 3 tablespoons. Add butter, one piece at a time, whisking constantly until the sauce is consistency of hollandaise. Lift the pan from heat occasionally to keep mixture from overheating. Whisk in the herbs, salt, and pepper.

Variations. Substitute flavored red wine, sherry, champagne, rice, or balsamic vinegar for the white wine vinegar. Fruit-flavored vinegars, such as raspberry, are especially good. When using a heavier vinegar, such as a red wine one, use with grilled meats and fish like salmon, swordfish, or halibut.

Mustard-Dill Sauce

Use with steamed vegetables or grilled chicken or fish.

Yield: ¾ cup

- ½ cup fresh dill
- ¼ cup Dijon mustard
- 3 tablespoons dill white wine vinegar
- 3 tablespoons plain nonfat yogurt
- 1 tablespoon honey
- ½ cup extra-virgin olive oil

In a blender or food processor, combine dill, mustard, vinegar, yogurt, and honey until well blended. With the motor running, slowly add the oil in a thin stream. Blend until sauce is thick and smooth. Place in a covered bowl and refrigerate before serving.

Sorrel Sauce

Use this fresh, tangy sauce that needs no cooking as a nonfat partner to lightly steamed vegetables.

Yield: 1 cup

- 1 cup fresh sorrel
- 2 cups apple, cored, peeled, and diced
- ¼ cup lemon thyme white wine or cider vinegar
- 1 tablespoon honey

In a food processor combine all ingredients until smooth. Serve immediately.

Variation. Cook the sorrel, apples, and vinegar together over medium heat until the apples are soft, or about 10 minutes. Puree in a blender. Return to low heat and stir in the honey and 2 tablespoons butter. Cook until warm and butter is melted.

Roasted Pepper Sauce

Serve over pasta, grains, chicken, fish, or vegetables.

Yield: 2 cups

- 3 sweet red peppers (or enough to make 2 cups), roasted, peeled, cored, and seeded
- ⅓ cup pine nuts or blanched, sliced or slivered almonds, toasted
- 1 clove garlic

⅓ cup extra-virgin olive oil

⅓ cup basil sherry vinegar

2 tablespoons fresh basil, minced

2 tablespoons fresh chives, minced

½ teaspoon salt

Combine all ingredients in a blender or food processor and process until smooth
Use immediately or store in a covered jar or nonreactive bowl in the refrigerator.

Black Bean Sauce

Serve over steamed or stir-fried vegetables or grains.

Yield: 1½ cups

One 15- or 16-ounce can black beans,
rinsed and drained

1 clove garlic

2 tablespoons extra-virgin olive oil

1 tablespoon Dijon mustard

¼ cup cilantro sherry vinegar

¼ cup green onion, minced

1 tablespoon fresh cilantro, minced

¼ cup water

½ teaspoon hot red pepper sauce

Combine all ingredients in a blender or food processor and process until smooth.
Use immediately or store in a covered jar or nonreactive bowl in the refrigerator.

Curry Sauce

Curry paste can be substituted for curry powder in recipes.
As curry powder tends to lose flavor once opened, this is a good
way of preserving it.

Yield: 1½ cups

3 tablespoons untoasted sesame oil

1 cup curry powder

1 cup spice white wine vinegar

1 tablespoon sugar

Heat oil in heavy skillet over medium heat. Stir in curry powder, lower heat, and
warm for 5 minutes, stirring constantly. Stir in vinegar and sugar, until smooth.
Remove from heat, cool, and store in a tightly covered jar in the refrigerator.

ALMOND-PEPPER SAUCE

This sauce with Spanish origins can be used to garnish seafood stews, grilled tuna or other fish, or steamed vegetables.

Yield: 2 cups

- 1 cup blanched, sliced or slivered almonds, toasted
- 2 large egg yolks, hard-cooked
- 2 cloves garlic
- ½ cup sweet red pepper, roasted, peeled, cored, and seeded
- 1 small fresh hot red pepper, cored and seeded
- 2 tablespoons fresh parsley, minced
- ¼ cup garlic red wine vinegar
- ¾ cup extra-virgin olive oil
- 3 tablespoons boiling water

In a food processor or blender, combine almonds, egg yolks, garlic, sweet and hot peppers, parsley, and vinegar. Process until smooth. With the machine running, slowly add the olive oil in a thin stream, and then the boiling water. Store in a covered nonreactive bowl in the refrigerator. Serve chilled or at room temperature.

SWEET-AND-SOUR SAUCE

Use this for dipping egg rolls or poured over stir-fried dishes.

Yield: 1½ cups

- 1 cup pineapple juice
- ¼ cup water
- ¼ cup ginger or garlic chives rice wine vinegar
- ¼ cup packed light brown sugar
- 2 tablespoons soy sauce
- 1 tablespoon tomato paste
- 1 clove garlic, minced
- 1 tablespoon fresh ginger, minced
- 1 tablespoon cornstarch mixed in 2 tablespoons water

In a small, heavy, nonreactive saucepan, combine pineapple juice, water, vinegar, sugar, soy sauce, tomato paste, garlic, and ginger. Place over medium heat and bring to a boil. Reduce heat to low and simmer for 5 minutes. Stir in cornstarch mixture and simmer until sauce thickens and clears. Serve warm or at room temperature, or chill for later use.

Béarnaise Sauce

Although this rich French sauce is usually served over steaks, try it with roasts and hamburgers as well as vegetables and fish.

Yield: 1 cup

- ¼ cup tarragon white wine vinegar
- 2 tablespoons shallot, minced
- 2 tablespoons fresh tarragon, minced
- 2 tablespoons fresh chervil, minced (optional)
- 8 black peppercorns
- 1 bay leaf
- 3 large egg yolks
- ¼ cup vegetable stock
- ¾ cup butter

In a small, heavy, nonreactive saucepan, combine vinegar, shallots, tarragon, chervil, peppercorns, and bay leaf. Bring to a boil over medium heat. Reduce heat to low and simmer mixture until reduced by half. Strain and reserve the liquid. Combine the egg yolks and the stock and pour into the top of a double boiler over simmering water. Stirring constantly, add the butter a half tablespoon at a time. When the mixture has thickened, stir in the reserved liquid. Serve immediately.

Basil Cream Sauce

Serve over pasta, steamed vegetables, or grilled chicken or fish.

Yield: 2½ cups

- 8 ounces low-fat cream cheese at room temperature
- 1 cup pine nuts, toasted
- 1 cup fresh basil
- 1 cup fresh parsley
- ½ cup Parmesan cheese, freshly grated
- ¼ cup basil white wine vinegar
- ¼ cup extra-virgin olive oil
- ¼ cup plain nonfat yogurt
- 1 teaspoon hot red pepper sauce
- ½ teaspoon salt

In a blender or food processor, combine all ingredients and process until smooth. Serve immediately or refrigerate and bring to room temperature before serving.

Parsley-Lemon Basil Sauce

Serve over pasta, steamed vegetables, or grilled chicken or fish.

Yield: 1 cup

- 2 cups fresh parsley
- ½ cup fresh lemon basil
- ¼ cup fresh garlic chives
- ¼ cup pecans, toasted
- 2 tablespoons Parmesan cheese, freshly grated
- ½ cup vegetable stock
- ¼ cup parsley, lemon basil, or garlic chives white wine vinegar
- ¼ cup extra-virgin olive oil
- ½ teaspoon salt
- ½ teaspoon freshly ground black pepper

In a blender or food processor, combine all ingredients and process until smooth. Serve immediately or refrigerate and bring to room temperature before serving.

Fresh Tomato Sauce

Serve over pasta or grilled fish or chicken. Use plum tomatoes or any meaty variety.

Yield: 3 cups

- 2 cups tomatoes, peeled, seeded, and chopped
- ¼ cup mixed-herb red wine vinegar
- ½ cup fresh parsley, minced
- 2 tablespoons fresh basil, minced
- 2 tablespoons fresh spearmint, minced
- 2 cloves garlic, minced
- 1 teaspoon salt
- ½ teaspoon freshly ground black pepper
- ½ cup extra-virgin olive oil

In large nonreactive bowl, combine all ingredients except olive oil. Add oil in a thin stream, whisking continually until it is well combined. Serve at room temperature.

HOT PEPPER SAUCE

*Very, very hot, use this sauce sparingly as a condiment
for Caribbean dishes or other foods.*

Yield: 2 cups

- 6 red habañero peppers, cored and seeded
- 2 cups onion, chopped
- 2 cloves garlic
- 4 allspice berries, crushed
- ½ teaspoon ground cumin
- 1 tablespoon tomato paste
- 2 cups garlic cider vinegar

In a food processor, combine peppers, onion, garlic, allspice, and cumin and
process until fine. In a nonreactive saucepan, combine the pepper mixture with
the tomato paste and vinegar. Bring to a boil over medium heat, stirring occasionally. Cool, bottle, and refrigerate.

GREEN SAUCE

*Serve with steamed vegetables, grilled or roasted meats,
or salad greens.*

Yield: 1¼ cups

- 1 cup fresh parsley
- ¼ cup fresh chives
- ¼ cup green onion, sliced
- 2 tablespoons fresh spearmint
- 1 tablespoon fresh tarragon
- 1 tablespoon fresh chervil
- 1 clove garlic
- 1 tablespoon capers
- 2 anchovy fillets
- ¼ cup mixed-herb red or white wine vinegar
- 1 large egg, hard-cooked and peeled
- ½ teaspoon freshly ground black pepper
- ⅔ cup extra-virgin olive oil

In a food processor, combine all ingredients except olive oil. Process until
smooth. With the machine running, slowly add the oil in a thin stream.
Serve chilled or at room temperature. Store in a tightly covered container
in the refrigerator.

Barbecue Sauce

Yield: 1 pint

- 1 cup tomato puree
- ¼ cup onion, finely chopped
- ¼ cup sweet red pepper, cored, seeded, and chopped
- 1 clove garlic, minced
- ¼ cup dark molasses
- ¼ cup packed light brown sugar
- ½ cup mixed-herb or garlic red wine vinegar
- 3 tablespoons Worcestershire sauce
- 2 tablespoons lemon juice
- 2 teaspoons dry English mustard
- 1 teaspoon fresh thyme, minced
- 1 teaspoon salt
- 1 teaspoon chili powder
- 1 teaspoon ground cayenne pepper or hot red pepper sauce
- ½ teaspoon freshly ground black pepper
- 1 bay leaf

Combine all ingredients in a blender or food processor and process until smooth. Transfer to a heavy nonreactive saucepan. Bring to a boil over medium heat, then reduce heat to low and simmer for 15 minutes. Refrigerate in a tightly covered jar.

Summer Vegetable Salsa

Serve over pasta or with grilled meats, fish, or poultry.

Yield: 4 cups

- 3 cups tomatoes, peeled, seeded, and diced
- 1 cup cucumber, peeled, seeded, and finely chopped
- ½ cup corn kernels, cooked
- ½ cup green onion, thinly sliced
- ½ cup green pepper, cored, seeded, and diced
- ¼ cup celery, diced
- ½ cup cilantro red wine vinegar

¼　cup extra-virgin olive oil

　¼　cup fresh cilantro, minced

　2　tablespoons horseradish, grated
　　　(fresh or preserved in vinegar)

　2　tablespoons fresh parsley, minced

　2　cloves garlic, minced

　1　small hot green pepper, cored, seeded, and minced

　1　teaspoon salt

　½　teaspoon ground cumin

　½　teaspoon freshly ground black pepper

Combine all ingredients in a large nonreactive bowl. Serve chilled.

Variation. To preserve for future use, place all ingredients in a large heavy nonreactive saucepan and bring to a boil over medium heat. Reduce heat to low and simmer for 20 minutes, stirring frequently. To freeze, let the mixture cool, then put into pint freezer containers and freeze. Or, follow directions on page 125 for boiling-water method of preserving.

Tomatillo Salsa

Yield: 3½ cups

　2　pounds fresh tomatillos

　½　cup cilantro or chive blossom white wine or rice vinegar

　½　teaspoon salt

　¼　cup green onion, sliced

　½　cup fresh cilantro

　2　fresh green jalapeño peppers, cored and seeded

　2　cloves garlic

　1　teaspoon sugar

Peel husks off tomatillos. Rinse in cold water. In a heavy nonreactive saucepan, bring vinegar and salt to a boil over medium heat. Add tomatillos and cover. Cook until softened, or about 5 minutes. Remove from heat and transfer to a food processor or blender with remaining ingredients. Process briefly to a puree. Store in a tightly covered container in the refrigerator. Use within 5 days.

MUSTARDS

xperiment with different vinegars and herbs, using either a single herb or a mixture, matching the vinegar to the fresh herbs or using complementary ones. Some of the herbs to try with mustards include the basils, burnet, celery seed, chervil, chives, cilantro leaves or seeds, dill leaves or seeds, fennel leaves or seeds, garlic chives, horseradish, hot peppers, parsley, rosemary, tarragon, and the thymes. Be sure to try fruit vinegars, too, matching vinegar and fruit juice. Consider raspberry and other bramble fruits, blueberry, and cranberry.

MUSTARD I

Yield: 2 cups

- ½ cup light or dark mustard seeds
- ¼ cup dry English mustard
- ¾ cup herb or other flavored vinegar
- ⅔ cup water, wine, beer, or fruit juice
- ¼ cup fresh herbs, minced, or 2 tablespoons herb seeds, ground
- 2 tablespoons honey or 3 tablespoons white or packed brown sugar
- 1 teaspoon salt

Combine mustard seeds, dry mustard, vinegar, and other liquid in a nonreactive bowl. Let sit for 4 hours, uncovered, stirring occasionally. Transfer to a blender or food processor. Process to the desired texture, from slightly coarse to creamy. Pour into the top of a double boiler over simmering water. Stir in remaining ingredients. Cook for 10 minutes, or until thickened, stirring often. Mustard will be thicker when cooled. Pour into sterilized jars, cap tightly, and store in the refrigerator. Wait several days before using to allow flavors to blend.

MUSTARD II

Yield: 2 cups

- 1 cup dry English mustard
- 1 cup herb or other flavored vinegar
- 3 tablespoons water, wine, beer, or fruit juice
- ¼ cup fresh herbs, minced
- 2 tablespoons honey or 3 tablespoons white or packed brown sugar
- 1 teaspoon salt

Combine dry mustard, vinegar, and other liquid in a nonreactive bowl. Let sit for 4 hours uncovered, stirring occasionally. Pour into the top of a double boiler over simmering water. Stir in remaining ingredients. Cook for 10 minutes, or until thickened, stirring often. Mustard will be thicker when cooled. Pour into sterilized jars, cap tightly, and store in the refrigerator. Wait several days before using to allow flavors to blend.

MUSTARD III

Yield: 2 cups

- 1 cup dry English mustard
- 1 cup herb or other flavored vinegar
- ½ cup water, wine, beer, or fruit juice
- ½ cup packed light brown sugar or ¼ cup honey
- ¼ cup fresh herbs, minced
- 1 teaspoon salt
- 3 large eggs, lightly beaten

Combine the dry mustard, vinegar, and other liquid in a nonreactive bowl. Let sit for 4 hours uncovered, stirring occasionally.Pour into the top of a double boiler over simmering water. Stir in the remaining ingredients. Cook for 10 minutes, or until thickened, stirring often. Mustard will be thicker when cooled. Pour into sterilized jars, cap tightly, and store in the refrigerator. Wait several days before using to allow flavors to blend.

Basil-Shallot-Red Wine Mustard

Yield: 2 cups

- ¼ cup light or dark mustard seeds
- ½ cup dry English mustard
- ⅔ cup dry red wine
- ⅔ cup basil-shallot red wine vinegar
- ⅓ cup water
- 1 tablespoon shallot, minced
- 1 tablespoon honey or
  2 tablespoons packed light brown sugar
- 1 teaspoon salt
- ¼ teaspoon ground allspice
- 3 tablespoons fresh basil, minced

Combine the mustard seeds, dry mustard, red wine, vinegar, and water in a nonreactive bowl and stir until smooth. Let sit, for 4 hours, uncovered, stirring occasionally. Transfer to a blender or food processor. Process to the desired consistency, from slightly coarse to creamy. Pour into the top of a double boiler over simmering water. Stir in the remaining ingredients. Cook for about 10 minutes, or until thickened, stirring often. Mustard will be thicker when cooled. Stir in the basil. Pour into sterilized jars, cap tightly, and store in the refrigerator. Wait several days before using to allow flavors to blend.

Sherry-Thyme Mustard

Yield: 1½ cups

- ½ cup light or dark mustard seeds
- 2 tablespoons dry English mustard
- ½ cup dry sherry
- ½ cup thyme sherry vinegar
- 2 tablespoons honey
- 2 tablespoons fresh thyme, minced
- 2 teaspoons salt

Combine the mustard seeds, dry mustard, sherry, and vinegar in a nonreactive bowl. Let sit for 4 hours, uncovered, stirring occasionally. Transfer to a blender or food processor. Process to the desired texture, from slightly coarse to creamy. Pour into the top of a double boiler over simmering water. Stir in remaining ingredients. Cook for 10 minutes, or until thickened, stirring often. Mustard will be thicker when cooled. Pour into sterilized jars, cap tightly, and store in the refrigerator. Wait several days before using to allow flavors to blend.

Horseradish Mustard

Yield: 2 cups

- 1 cup dry English mustard
- 1 cup horseradish white wine vinegar
- ¼ cup water or dry white wine
- 2 tablespoons horseradish, grated
  (fresh or preserved in vinegar)
- 1 tablespoon honey or 2 tablespoons sugar
- 1 teaspoon salt
- 2 cloves garlic, minced
- ½ teaspoon freshly ground black pepper
- ½ teaspoon hot red pepper sauce
- ¼ teaspoon ground allspice

Combine the dry mustard, vinegar, and water or wine in a nonreactive bowl. Let sit for 4 hours, uncovered, stirring occasionally. Pour into the top of a double boiler over simmering water. Stir in remaining ingredients. Cook for 10 minutes, or until the mixture has thickened, stirring often. Mustard will be thicker when cooled. Pour into sterilized jars, cap tightly, and store in the refrigerator. Wait several days before using to allow flavors to blend.

Tarragon-Green Peppercorn Mustard

Yield: 1 cup

- ¼ cup light or dark mustard seeds
- ⅓ cup tarragon white wine vinegar
- ⅓ cup water
- ¼ cup dry white wine
- 1 tablespoon fresh tarragon, minced
- 1 tablespoon green peppercorns, crushed
- 1 tablespoon honey or 2 tablespoons sugar
- 1 teaspoon salt
- ⅛ teaspoon ground cloves

Combine mustard seeds, vinegar, water, and wine in a bowl. Let sit for 4 hours, uncovered, stirring occasionally. Transfer to a blender or food processor. Process to the desired consistency, from slightly coarse to creamy. Pour into the top of a double boiler over simmering water. Stir in the remaining ingredients. Cook for 10 minutes, or until thickened, stirring often. Mustard will be thicker when cooled. Pour into sterilized jars, cap tightly, and store in the refrigerator. Wait several days before using to allow flavors to blend.

BEER-SPICE MUSTARD

Yield: 1½ cups

- 1 cup dry English mustard
- 1 cup mixed-spice malt vinegar
- ¼ cup beer
- ¼ cup sugar
- ¼ cup packed light brown sugar
- 1 teaspoon salt
- 1 teaspoon caraway seeds
- ½ teaspoon ground ginger
- ½ teaspoon ground cloves
- ½ teaspoon ground cinnamon
- 2 large eggs, lightly beaten

Combine the dry mustard, vinegar, and beer in a nonreactive bowl. Let sit for 4 hours, uncovered, stirring occasionally. Pour into the top of a double boiler over simmering water. Stir in remaining ingredients. Cook for 10 minutes, or until the mixture has thickened, stirring often. Mustard will be thicker when cooled. Pour into sterilized jars, cap tightly, and store in the refrigerator. Wait several days before using to allow flavors to blend.

KETCHUPS

Our endemic tomato-based ketchup, so necessary for french fries, hamburgers, and hot dogs, is most closely identified with Asian origins, although similar spicy condiments have been around at least since Roman times. *Ketsiap* in China, *kechap* in Malaysia, and *ketjap* in Indonesia are basically brined fish condiments. Seventeenth-century British sailors brought these back to the mother country, where they came to be made from everything from green walnuts to mushrooms. North American colonists made them primarily with tomatoes, although other fruits were also used. Essentially, today, ketchups are cooked sauces used as a condiment, made with fruits or vegetables, vinegar, sugar, and spices.

QUICK TOMATO KETCHUP

Yield: Two 13- or 14-ounce bottles

- 3½ cups (28 ounces) canned tomato sauce
- ⅓ cup honey
- ⅓ cup lovage cider vinegar
- 2 tablespoons onion, minced
- 1 clove garlic, minced
- 1 teaspoon salt
- ½ teaspoon freshly ground black pepper
- ½ teaspoon ground mustard
- ⅛ teaspoon ground cayenne pepper
- ⅛ teaspoon ground allspice
- ⅛ teaspoon ground cloves
- ⅛ teaspoon ground coriander seeds

In a large nonreactive saucepan, combine all ingredients and place over low heat. Stirring frequently, simmer until the consistency of commercial ketchup, or about 30 minutes. Pour into hot, sterilized ketchup bottles and refrigerate.

Old-Fashioned Tomato Ketchup

Yield: 8 half-pints

   4 quarts plum or other meaty tomatoes, peeled, cored, and chopped
 1½ cups onion, chopped
   ½ cup sweet red pepper, cored, seeded, and chopped
   ¼ cup celery, chopped
   2 cloves garlic, minced
 1½ cups garlic or mixed-spice cider vinegar
   ½ cup packed dark brown sugar
   ¼ cup sugar
   2 teaspoons non-iodized salt
   2 teaspoons mustard seeds
   2 teaspoons whole allspice berries
   2 teaspoons whole black peppercorns
   2 teaspoons whole coriander seeds
   1 teaspoon whole cloves
   ½ teaspoon whole celery seeds
   ½ teaspoon whole cardamom seeds, husks removed
   ½ teaspoon dried hot red pepper flakes
      One 3-inch cinnamon stick, broken
   1 bay leaf

In a large, heavy nonreactive kettle, combine tomatoes, onion, sweet pepper, celery, and garlic. Bring to a boil over medium-high heat, then reduce heat to medium and simmer until vegetables are very soft, or about 45 minutes, stirring frequently. Put through a food mill, repeating, if desired, for a very smooth consistency.

Wash the kettle and return pureed tomato mixture to it. Stir in the vinegar, sugars, and salt. Place the remaining ingredients in a muslin spice bag or muslin square and securely tie. Add to the tomato mixture. Simmer over low heat until reduced by at least one-half and the mixture is the thickness desired. Remove the spice bag. Follow standard directions for the boiling-water method of preserving, page 125.

Mushroom Ketchup

Use this as a condiment for roasts, steaks, hamburgers,
and chops as well as a seasoning for sauces, gravies,
and salad dressings.

Yield: 4 to 5 half-pints

- 3 pounds mushrooms, thinly sliced
- 2 tablespoons non-iodized salt
- 1 cup onion, chopped
- 1 small hot red pepper, cored, seeded, and chopped
- 2 cloves garlic, minced
- 1 tablespoon fresh thyme
- 1 tablespoon fresh parsley
- 1 tablespoon fresh marjoram
- ½ teaspoon ground allspice
- ½ teaspoon ground ginger
- ¼ teaspoon ground cloves
- 1 bay leaf
- 1 cup mixed-herb or mixed-spice sherry vinegar
- 2 tablespoons honey

Put the mushrooms and salt in a nonreactive bowl, mixing thoroughly. Cover and let mixture stand at room temperature for 24 hours, stirring occasionally. Puree the mushrooms in a food processor or food mill, then pour into a large heavy nonreactive kettle.

Combine all remaining ingredients except the bay leaf in a blender and process until smooth. Stir into the pureed mushrooms, mixing well. Add the bay leaf. Place over medium-high heat and bring to a boil. Reduce the heat to low and simmer, uncovered and stirring frequently, for 1 to 2 hours, or until the ketchup is very thick. Remove the bay leaf. Follow standard directions for the boiling-water method of preserving, page 125.

Peach Ketchup

Yield: 4 to 5 half-pints

- 4 pounds peaches, peeled, pitted, and chopped
- 1 cup onion, chopped
- 1 pint cinnamon or anise basil white wine or rice vinegar
- 1 teaspoon non-iodized salt
- 1 cup packed light brown sugar
- 1 teaspoon anise seeds
- 1 teaspoon mustard seeds
- 1 teaspoon whole black peppercorns
- One 3-inch cinnamon stick, broken
- 3 quarter-size pieces of fresh ginger
- ½ teaspoon whole cloves
- ½ teaspoon whole allspice berries

In a large, heavy nonreactive kettle, combine the peaches, onion, vinegar, salt, and sugar. Place the remaining ingredients in a small muslin spice bag or a square of muslin and tie tightly. Add to the peach mixture. Bring to a boil over medium-high heat, then reduce heat to low and simmer, covered but stirring frequently, for 30 minutes or until the peaches are very soft. Remove the spice bag and transfer to a food processor or blender and puree. Return the puree to the rinsed-out pan with the spice bag and continue to simmer, uncovered and stirring, until very thick, or about another 30 minutes to 1 hour. Remove the spice bag. Follow standard directions for the boiling-water method of preserving, page 125.

Cranberry Ketchup

Yield: 6 half-pints

- 2 cups onion, chopped
- 4 cups water
- Four 1 x 3-inch strips fresh orange zest
- 6 sprigs fresh orange mint
- 8 cups cranberries, fresh or frozen
- 1 cup cranberry-orange white wine or rice vinegar
- 1 cup packed light brown sugar
- 1 cup honey
- 1½ teaspoons non-iodized salt
- One 3-inch cinnamon stick, broken

1 teaspoon whole allspice berries

1 teaspoon whole cloves

3 quarter-size slices fresh ginger

In a large, heavy nonreactive kettle, combine the onion, water, orange zest, and orange mint sprigs. Cover and bring to a boil over medium-high heat, reduce heat to low and simmer until onion is softened, or about 10 minutes. Add the cranberries and bring the mixture to a boil. Stirring frequently, simmer until the berries are very soft, or about 15 minutes. Puree half the mixture at a time in a blender, food processor, or food mill. Return the puree to the rinsed-out kettle and add the vinegar, sugar, honey, and salt. Place the remaining ingredients in a small muslin spice bag or a square of muslin and tie tightly. Add to the cranberry mixture. Place over medium heat and bring to a boil, stirring frequently. Reduce heat to low and cook until very thick, or about 30 minutes. Remove the spice bag. Follow standard directions for the boiling-water method of preserving, page 125.

Concord Grape Ketchup

Other American "fox grapes" can be substituted for the Concords, including Delaware and Catawbas. Southerners can substitute Muscadines.

Yield: 4 half-pints

2 pounds Concord grapes, stemmed

3 cups water

2 cups packed light brown sugar

1 pint mixed-spice cider vinegar

1 teaspoon non-iodized salt

One 3-inch cinnamon stick, broken

1 teaspoon whole allspice berries

1 teaspoon whole cloves

1 teaspoon whole black peppercorns

2 quarter-size slices fresh ginger

In a large, heavy nonreactive kettle, combine the grapes and water. Bring to a boil over medium heat, then reduce heat to low and simmer until grapes are tender, or about 15 minutes. Run through a food mill and discard the seeds. Rinse the kettle and return the pulp to it with the sugar, vinegar, and salt. Place the remaining ingredients in a small muslin spice bag or a square of muslin and tie tightly. Add to the grape mixture. Place over medium heat and bring to a boil, stirring frequently. Reduce heat to low and cook until very thick, or about 30 to 45 minutes. Remove the spice bag. Follow standard directions for the boiling-water method of preserving, page 125.

PICKLES, RELISHES, AND OTHER PRESERVED FOODS

ny of your favorite pickle, relish, or other home-canned food recipes using vinegar can be uniquely yours with flavored vinegars. Feel free to experiment with different combinations of herbs and spices as well as other flavorings with the various vinegars. Just be sure that the vinegar you are using is at least 5 percent acidity or higher. Never use homemade vinegar with its unknown acidity. Whenever a recipe calls for cucumbers, make sure to choose cucumbers that have not been waxed. Half-pint jars may be substituted for pint jars when desired.

STANDARD DIRECTIONS FOR BOILING-WATER METHOD OF PRESERVING

1. Pour, ladle, or pack the prepared ingredients into clean, hot half-pint or pint jars, leaving ¼-inch space at the top.

2. Wipe the rims, put on two-piece lids, and fasten the screw bands.

3. Put the jars on a rack in a deep kettle half full of boiling water and add more boiling water to cover the lids by 2 inches.

4. Cover the pot, bring to a hard boil, and boil for 15 minutes, lowering heat, if necessary. Remove the jars from the boiling water.

5. Cool, remove bands, label, and store.

6. Let the flavors blend for at least a month before using. Refrigerate after opening.

Garlic-Dill Pickles

Yield: 6 pints

>About 4 pounds thin, straight 4-inch pickling cucumbers
6 cloves garlic
6 dill flower heads and six 6-inch leaves fresh dill
6 small fresh or dried hot red peppers (optional)
6 large fresh grape leaves
1 quart dill or garlic cider vinegar
1 quart water
½ cup non-iodized salt

Wash cucumbers and place in a bowl of cold water. Cover and refrigerate for 12 hours. In each clean, sterilized canning jar, place a garlic clove, a dill flower and leaf, grape leaf, optional hot pepper, and enough cucumbers to fill. In a large nonreactive kettle, combine vinegar, water, and salt. Bring to a boil over high heat and stir until salt is dissolved. Follow the standard directions for boiling-water method of preserving, page 125.

Hot-and-Sweet Pickles

Yield: 6 pints

>4 quarts plus 1 cup water
1 cup non-iodized pickling salt
4 pounds pickling cucumbers, cut into ½-inch slices
3 cups hot pepper cider vinegar
1½ cups packed light brown sugar
¼ cup fresh ginger, grated
3 tablespoons dried hot red pepper flakes
2 tablespoons mustard seeds
1 tablespoon celery seeds
1 tablespoon whole cloves
One 3-inch cinnamon stick
2 cloves garlic

In a large bowl, combine 4 quarts water and salt. Place cucumbers in the brine. Cover and refrigerate for 12 hours. Drain the cucumbers and rinse under running cold water, and drain again. In a large nonreactive kettle, combine 1 cup water, vinegar, and sugar. Combine the remaining ingredients in a muslin spice bag or muslin square, tie securely and add to the vinegar mixture. Bring to a boil over high heat, stirring until sugar is dissolved. Add the drained cucumbers and cook for 5 minutes, stirring constantly. Follow standard directions for boiling-water method of preserving, page 125.

Bread-and-Butter Pickles

Yield: 6 pints

- 8 cups pickling cucumbers, cut into ¼-inch slices
- ½ cup non-iodized salt
  Crushed or cracked ice
- 1 quart mixed-spice cider, malt, or red or white wine vinegar
- 3 cups sugar
- 3 tablespoons mustard seeds
- 1 tablespoon celery seeds
- 1 teaspoon turmeric
- 1 teaspoon whole black peppercorns
- ½ teaspoon ground cloves
- ½ teaspoon ground ginger
- 2 cups onion, sliced

In a large nonreactive bowl, combine cucumbers, salt, and ice. Let stand for 3 hours, then drain thoroughly. In a large nonreactive kettle, combine vinegar, sugar, mustard seeds, celery seeds, turmeric, peppercorns, cloves, and ginger. Bring to a boil over medium-high heat. Reduce heat to low and simmer for 5 minutes. Add the cucumber and sliced onion. Increase heat to medium-high, bring mixture to a boil, and cook for 3 minutes. Follow standard directions for boiling-water method of preserving, page 125.

Sweet Onion Preserves

Yield: 4 half-pints

- ½ cup extra-virgin olive oil
- 8 cups sweet onion, thinly sliced (about 3 pounds)
- 1 cup packed light brown sugar
- ⅔ cup tarragon white wine vinegar
- 1 cup dry white wine
- ¼ cup fresh tarragon, minced
- 1 teaspoon freshly ground white pepper

Warm the oil in a large, heavy nonreactive saucepan over medium heat. Stir in the onion and sugar. Reduce heat to low, cover, cook, stirring occasionally, for 30 minutes. Add the vinegar and wine and cook, uncovered, for 30 minutes or until the mixture is thick, stirring occasionally. Stir in the tarragon and pepper. Follow the standard directions for boiling-water method of preserving, page 125.

Pickled Peppers

The sweet pepper variety 'Jingle Bells' is a good one to use for this recipe, as the mature fruit is about 2 inches in diameter.

Yield: 3 quarts

12–18	small to medium whole green or red sweet peppers
1	cup plus 2 tablespoons non-iodized salt
1	gallon plus 1 pint water
10	cups green cabbage, finely shredded
2	cups onion, finely shredded
¼	cup mustard seeds
¼	cup horseradish, grated (fresh or preserved in vinegar)
2	tablespoons celery seeds
1	teaspoon freshly ground black pepper
1	teaspoon ground cloves
1	cup sugar
1	quart mixed-spice or horseradish cider, malt, or whitewine vinegar

Cut off the top quarter from the peppers and remove the seeds and ribs without breaking the peppers. Reserve the tops. In a large nonreactive bowl, put the peppers and tops and cover with 1 cup salt and 1 gallon water. Cover and refrigerate for 12 hours. Drain, rinse under running cold water, and drain again. In a large nonreactive bowl, combine cabbage, onion, mustard seeds, horseradish, celery seeds, black pepper, cloves, ½ cup of the sugar, and 2 tablespoons salt. Stuff the peppers with the cabbage mixture, cover with the tops, securing with wooden toothpicks or kitchen string.

In a heavy nonreactive saucepan, combine vinegar, 2 cups water, and ½ cup sugar. Bring to a boil over medium-high heat, stirring until the sugar is dissolved. Pack the peppers into hot, sterilized jars. Pour the hot vinegar mixture over the top, leaving ¼-inch headspace. Continue with steps 2–6 of the standard directions for boiling-water method of preserving, page 125.

Pickled Green Beans with Savory

Yield: 6 pints

3	pounds green beans
1	quart savory white wine vinegar
1	quart water
¼	cup non-iodized salt
1	tablespoon sugar
	Six 3-inch sprigs fresh summer savory

Remove the stem ends of the beans. Cut the beans to fit into the canning jars vertically, allowing ½ inch of headspace at the top. Fill the jars with the beans, putting a sprig of savory in each. In a heavy nonreactive saucepan, combine the vinegar, water, salt, and sugar. Bring to a boil over medium-high heat. Pour the hot liquid into the jars, leaving ¼-inch space at the top. Continue with steps 2–6 of the standard directions for boiling-water method of preserving, page 125, processing for 10 minutes.

PICKLED ASPARAGUS WITH TARRAGON

Yield: 3 pints

1½ pounds asparagus spears
1½ cups water
 ½ cup sugar
  1 teaspoon non-iodized salt
 ½ teaspoon freshly ground black pepper
1½ cups tarragon white wine vinegar
     Three 3-inch sprigs fresh tarragon

Cut off the tough portion of the asparagus stalks. Prepare the asparagus by either cutting into 2-inch lengths or cutting all stems to the height of the canning jar, less ½ inch. Blanch in boiling water, 2 minutes for pieces or 3 minutes for stalks. Immediately drain and immerse in ice water. Cool thoroughly, then drain. In a heavy nonreactive saucepan, combine water, sugar, salt, and pepper. Bring to a boil over medium-high heat, stirring until sugar is dissolved. Remove from heat and stir in vinegar. Pack the asparagus into hot, sterilized canning jars. Add a sprig of tarragon to each jar. Cover with the hot vinegar solution, leaving ¼-inch space at the top. Continue with steps 2–6 of the directions for boiling-water method of preserving, page 125, processing for 10 minutes.

PICKLED CRANBERRIES WITH ORANGE AND MINT

Yield: 3 pints

  3 cups cranberry red or white wine vinegar
3½ cups sugar
1½ cups water
  2 tablespoons fresh orange zest
  7 cups cranberries
 ½ cup fresh mint, minced

In a large, heavy nonreactive kettle, combine vinegar, sugar, water, and orange zest. Bring the mixture to a boil over medium heat, stirring frequently. Reduce heat to low and simmer for 5 minutes, continuing to stir. Add the cranberries and cook for 5 to 7 minutes, or until skins have popped. Stir in the mint. Follow the standard directions for the boiling-water method of preserving, page 125.

Hot Pickled Okra with Dill

Yield: 6 pints

3–4 pounds of 2-inch okra pods

- 1 pint dill white wine vinegar
- 1 cup water
- ¼ cup non-iodized salt
- 6 cloves garlic
- 6 small red or green hot peppers

  Six 3-inch sprigs fresh dill or 6 teaspoons dill seeds
- 3 teaspoons mustard seeds

Trim the okra, leaving about ¼ inch of the stem end. In a heavy nonreactive saucepan, combine the vinegar, water, and salt. Bring to a boil over medium-high heat, stirring until salt is dissolved. Fill hot, sterilized canning jars with the okra pods. Include in each jar a garlic clove, hot pepper, dill sprig or 1 teaspoon dill seeds, and ½ teaspoon mustard seeds. Pour hot vinegar solution into each jar, leaving ½-inch headspace at the top. Continue with steps 2–6 of the standard directions for the boiling-water method of preserving, page 125.

Pickled Green Cherry Tomatoes with Herbs

Yield: 6 pints

- 1 quart basil white wine or sherry vinegar
- 1 pint water
- ¼ cup non-iodized salt
- 1 tablespoon sugar
- 3 quarts green cherry tomatoes

  Six 4-inch sprigs fresh lovage

  Six 4-inch sprigs fresh basil

  Six 4-inch sprigs fresh thyme
- 3 cloves garlic, cut in half
- 1½ teaspoons mustard seeds
- 1½ teaspoons whole black peppercorns
- 1½ teaspoons ground ginger

In a heavy nonreactive saucepan, combine vinegar, water, salt, and sugar. Bring to a boil over medium-high heat, stirring until salt is dissolved. Pierce each tomato several times with a toothpick or bamboo skewer. Pack each hot, sterilized canning jar with tomatoes, one lovage sprig, one basil sprig, one thyme sprig, one-half garlic clove, ¼ teaspoon mustard seeds, ¼ teaspoon black pepper-corns, and ¼ teaspoon ground ginger. Pour the hot vinegar solution into each jar, leaving ¼-inch space at the top. Continue with steps 2–6 of the standard directions for the boiling-water method of preserving, page 125.

Vegetable Relish

Yield: 6 pints

6	cups unwaxed, unpeeled cucumber, chopped
1	cup sweet green pepper, cored, seeded, and chopped
1	cup sweet red pepper, cored, seeded, and chopped
2	cups onion, chopped
1	cup celery, chopped
½	cup non-iodized salt
3	cups cabbage, finely chopped
1	quart mixed-spice sherry vinegar
1	cup packed light brown sugar
1	cup sugar
2	tablespoons mustard seeds
1	teaspoon celery seeds
1	teaspoon turmeric
1	teaspoon freshly ground black pepper
½	teaspoon ground cinnamon
½	teaspoon ground cloves
½	teaspoon ground allspice
½	teaspoon ground cayenne pepper

In a large nonreactive bowl, combine the cucumber, green and red pepper, onion, celery, and salt. Cover and refrigerate for 12 hours. Drain and return to the bowl. Mix in the cabbage. In a large, heavy nonreactive kettle, combine the vinegar, sugars, mustard seeds, celery seeds, turmeric, black pepper, cinnamon, cloves, allspice, and cayenne. Bring to a boil over medium-high heat. Stir in the vegetables. Stirring constantly, bring to a boil and cook for 5 minutes. Follow standard directions for boiling-water method of preserving, page 125.

ZUCCHINI RELISH

Yield: 6 pints

- 12 cups zucchini, grated
- 4 cups onion, grated
- 1 sweet red pepper, cored, seeded, and chopped
- 1 sweet green pepper, cored, seeded, and chopped
- ⅓ cup non-iodized salt
- 1 quart mixed-herb white wine or cider vinegar
- 4 cups sugar
- 1 tablespoon dry English mustard
- 2 teaspoons celery seeds
- 1 teaspoon freshly ground black pepper
- ½ teaspoon ground cinnamon
- ½ teaspoon ground nutmeg
- ½ teaspoon turmeric
- ¼ cup fresh parsley, minced
- 2 tablespoons fresh thyme, minced
- 2 tablespoons fresh marjoram, minced

In large nonreactive bowl, combine zucchini, onion, peppers, and salt. Cover and refrigerate 12 hours. Drain, rinse in running cold water, and drain again. In large, heavy nonreactive kettle, combine vinegar, sugar, mustard, celery seeds, black pepper, cinnamon, nutmeg, and turmeric. Bring to a boil over medium-high heat, stirring until sugar is dissolved. Add vegetables, reduce heat to low, and cook for 30 minutes, stirring frequently, or until mixture is very thick. Remove from heat and stir in parsley, thyme, and marjoram. Follow standard directions for boiling-water method of preserving, page 125.

CORN RELISH

Yield: 6 pints

- 10 cups corn kernels, cooked
- 2 cups onion, chopped
- 2 cups cabbage, finely chopped
- 1½ cups sweet red pepper, cored, seeded, and chopped
- 1½ cups sweet green pepper, cored, seeded, and chopped
- 1½ cups sugar
- 3 cups hot pepper white wine or cider vinegar
- 1 pint water
- 2 tablespoons mustard seeds
- 2 tablespoons non-iodized salt

1 tablespoon celery seeds

1 teaspoon turmeric

In a large, heavy nonreactive kettle combine all ingredients. Bring to a boil over medium heat, stirring constantly until sugar is dissolved. Reduce the heat to low and, stirring frequently, continue to cook for 20 to 30 minutes, or until vegetables are tender and liquid is thickened. Follow the standard directions for the boiling-water method of preserving, page 125.

PEPPER-ONION RELISH

Yield: 6 pints

6 cups sweet red pepper, cored, seeded, and chopped

6 cups sweet green pepper, cored, seeded, and chopped

½ cup jalapeño or other hot pepper, cored, seeded, and chopped (optional)

4 cups onion, finely chopped

3 cups cilantro white wine vinegar

2 cups sugar

3 tablespoons non-iodized salt

½ cup fresh cilantro, minced

In a large, heavy nonreactive kettle, combine pepper, onion, vinegar, sugar, and salt. Stirring frequently, bring to a boil over medium heat. Reduce heat to low, continue stirring, and simmer for 20 minutes. Stir in the cilantro. Follow the standard directions for the boiling-water method of preserving, page 125.

PICKLED CHERRIES WITH HYSSOP

Yield: 4 pints

2 pounds sweet cherries

Twelve 4-inch sprigs fresh hyssop

1 quart hyssop red wine vinegar

½ cup sugar

4 teaspoons non-iodized salt

Trim cherry stems to ½ inch, prick each cherry with a sterilized needle, remove any soft or blemished fruit, and remove any moisture from washing. Put 3 sprigs of hyssop into each pint jar. Fill hot, sterilized canning jars with cherries to within ½ inch of the top. In a heavy nonreactive saucepan, combine the vinegar, sugar, and salt. Bring to a boil over medium heat, stirring until the sugar and salt is dissolved. Pour the solution over the cherries, filling to within ½ inch of the top. Continue with steps 2–6 of the standard directions for the boiling-water method of preserving, page 125.

Pickled Grapes with Thyme

Yield: 4 pints

- 7 cups stemmed seedless grapes
- Sixteen 4-inch sprigs fresh thyme
- 3 cups thyme white wine vinegar
- ½ cup sugar
- 1 tablespoon non-iodized salt

Remove any moisture from the grapes. Put 4 sprigs of thyme into each pint jar. Fill clean, hot, sterilized canning jars with grapes to within ½ inch of the top. In a heavy nonreactive saucepan, combine the vinegar, sugar, and salt. Bring to a boil over medium heat, stirring until the sugar and salt are dissolved. Pour the solution over the grapes, filling to within ½ inch of the top. Continue with steps 2–6 of the standard directions for boiling-water method of preserving, page 125.

Chili Sauce

Yield: 6 pints

- 10 cups plum tomatoes, peeled, seeded, and diced
- 2 cups sweet red pepper, cored, seeded, and finely chopped
- 2 cups onion, finely chopped
- 1 cup celery, finely chopped
- 1 hot red pepper, cored, seeded, and minced
- 1 clove garlic, minced
- 1½ cups garlic red wine or cider vinegar
- 1 tablespoon non-iodized salt
- 1 teaspoon ground cinnamon
- 1 teaspoon dry English mustard
- ½ teaspoon ground cloves
- ½ teaspoon ground allspice
- ½ teaspoon freshly ground black pepper
- ⅔ cup sugar
- ⅓ cup packed light brown sugar

In a large, heavy nonreactive kettle, combine tomatoes, sweet pepper, onion, celery, hot pepper, garlic, vinegar, salt, cinnamon, mustard, cloves, allspice, and black pepper. Place over medium heat and bring to a boil, stirring constantly. Reduce heat to low and simmer, uncovered, for 1 hour. Stir in the sugars. Stir constantly until the sugar is dissolved. Simmer for another 30 minutes, or until mixture is as thick as desired. Follow the standard directions for the boiling-water method of preserving, page 125.

Pickled Crabapples with Spices

Yield: 4 pints

- 4 pounds crabapples
- 4 cups mixed-spiced red wine vinegar
- 2 cups sugar
- 1 cup water
- Three 3-inch cinnamon sticks
- 1 teaspoon whole cloves
- 1 teaspoon whole allspice berries

Trim crabapple stems to ½ inch and run a large sterilized needle through each. In a large, heavy nonreactive kettle, combine vinegar, sugar, and water. Place cinnamon, cloves, and allspice in a muslin spice bag or square, securely tie, and add to kettle. Bring to a boil over medium heat, stirring frequently, until the sugar is dissolved. Reduce heat to low and simmer for 10 minutes, stirring frequently. Add crabapples and simmer for 10 minutes. Remove spices. Ladle into clean, hot, sterilized canning jars, leaving ½-inch space at the top. Continue with steps 2–6 of the standard directions for the boiling-water method of preserving, page 125.

Cooked Tomato Salsa

Yield: 4 half-pints

- 4 cups tomatoes, peeled, seeded, and chopped
- 1 cup onion, chopped
- ⅓ cup fresh jalapeño pepper, cored, seeded, and minced
- 2 cloves garlic, minced
- ½ cup fresh cilantro, minced
- ¼ cup cilantro or garlic red wine vinegar
- 1 teaspoon non-iodized salt

Combine all ingredients in a large heavy, nonreactive saucepan. Place over medium heat and bring to a boil. Reduce heat and simmer for 20 minutes. Follow the standard directions for the boiling-water method of preserving, page 125.

Plum Sauce

This is a homemade version of the dipping sauce used with egg rolls and other Chinese food.

Yield: 8 half-pints

2¼ pounds red plums, pitted and chopped
(weight is before preparation)

2¼ pounds apricots, pitted and chopped
(weight is before preparation)

1 cup sweet red pepper, roasted, cored,
peeled, and chopped

2 hot red or green pepper, cored, seeded, and minced

1 pound sweet onion, chopped

4 cloves garlic, minced

5 cups ginger rice vinegar

1 pint water

1½ cups packed light brown sugar

1½ cups sugar

⅓ cup fresh ginger, minced

1 tablespoon dry English mustard

2 teaspoons non-iodized salt

½ teaspoon ground cinnamon

½ teaspoon ground nutmeg

½ teaspoon ground allspice

¼ teaspoon ground cloves

Combine all ingredients in a large, heavy nonreactive kettle. Place over medium heat and bring to a boil, stirring frequently. Reduce heat to low and simmer for 1½ hours, or until soft and thick, stirring frequently. Puree in batches in a blender or run through a food mill. Return to the rinsed kettle and simmer for 15 minutes. Follow the standard directions for the boiling-water method of preserving, page 125.

OVEN-DRIED TOMATOES

*Dried tomatoes add a richness to pastas, salads, sautéed
vegetables, and sauces. Most parts of the United States do
not have the hot dry air necessary to sun dry tomatoes. If you
have a dehydrator, you can readily use it for this recipe.
Lacking that, an oven is an adequate alternative.*

        Plum tomatoes
        Salt
        Flavored vinegar
        Olive oil

Cut the tomatoes in half and remove the stem end. Lay them cut side up on
nonreactive (non–aluminum) baking sheets. Lightly salt. Place in an oven with
a pilot light or on the lowest possible temperature. Drying time will depend on
the oven, humidity, and the tomatoes. They are dried when they are shriveled
and have a leathery, prune-like texture. Dip each tomato half in vinegar, shaking
off the excess, and then place in a sterilized canning jar. Pack each jar with
tomatoes, leaving ½-inch space at the top. Garlic or herbs, such as rosemary,
basil, or thyme, can be added to the jars. Completely cover the tomatoes with
olive oil. Store jars in the refrigerator.

GARLIC JAM

*This redolent condiment is perfect served at room
temperature with grilled meats and vegetables.*

Yield: 2 half-pints

    1 pound garlic cloves, minced
    1 cup thyme sherry vinegar
    ½ cup dry sherry
    1 cup sugar
    ¼ cup fresh thyme, minced

Combine all ingredients in a heavy nonreactive saucepan. Place over
medium-high heat, bring to a boil, then reduce heat to low. Simmer until the
garlic is soft and the mixture is thickened, or about 30 minutes. Follow the
standard directions for the boiling-water method of preserving, page 125.

Preserved Horseradish

This is a dual–purpose preparation. The horseradish is preserved for use in recipes (some examples are in the Sauces and Mustards sections of this book), and the vinegar makes a top-notch addition to salad dressings, marinades, and other foods.

Yield: 4 half-pint jars

2   pounds fresh horseradish, peeled and finely grated
1   cup white wine, apple cider, or malt vinegar

Fill hot, sterilized jars with grated horseradish. Fill to within ¼-inch of the top with vinegar. Attach two-piece canning jar lids and rings. Store in refrigerator.

Variations. Ginger can be grated and stored in the same manner. Combine with a tart fruit jam as a sauce for game and other meats.

Horseradish

When peeled, the thick brown taproot of horseradish yields a pungent off-white interior. With its sharp, biting flavor, horseradish is traditionally served with boiled or roasted beef, smoked fish, and egg salad, especially when combined in a vinegar-and-cream sauce. Use the intense flavor to enhance mayonnaise or spark lingonberry sauce for venison and a hollandaise for asparagus or salmon. A relative of mustard, horseradish is high in vitamin C and was at one time served in a cordial at inns and taverns to refresh weary travelers. It is thought by some to enhance appetite and promote hair growth.

Horseradish does not take to cooking well and is best used as a condiment or added to a dish at the end of cooking. Harvest one-year-old roots in the fall after weather cools. Although it can be stored in the refrigerator crisper or in dry sand, horseradish is most apt to be used with the frequency it deserves if grated, covered with vinegar, and stored in the refrigerator. A blender or food processor makes quick work of grating, but be careful when removing the lid, as the pungent vapors will have accumulated to staggering proportions.

CHAPTER 16

CHUTNEYS
AND SAMBALS

Sambals are condiments common throughout southern India, Indonesia, and Malaysia. They are a puree or paste that traditionally accompanies curry and similar dishes, made and eaten fresh anduncooked. Some of the most common ingredients include mangoes, cucumbers, cilantro, mint, ginger, hot green peppers, onion, garlic, and coconut, moistened with lemon or lime juice as well as vinegar.

Cooked chutneys are also customary accompaniments to Indian and similar cuisines. But don't overlook them as side dishes or flavorings for cold cuts and roasted meats, cheeses, sandwiches, and grilled meats, and for seasoning salad dressings. Cooked chutneys are usually hot, spicy-sweet mixtures of chopped fruits or vegetables—a combination pickle and preserve, sweet-and-sour. To make them, chopped fruits and vegetables are cooked with vinegar, sugar, and a selection of herbs and spices. They may be made mildly to very hot with chili peppers. The mixtures often include raisins, dried currants, and nuts. Cooked chutneys are a British invention of the colonials who governed India and are named after the Hindustani word for strong spices, *chatni*.

Fresh Mint-Cucumber Sambal

This a quickly prepared, uncooked sambal that is traditional with Indian food, especially a type of fritter called pakoras.

Yield: 2 cups

- 1 cup fresh mint leaves
- 1 medium cucumber, peeled, seeded, and chopped
- 1 cup nonfat or low-fat plain yogurt or low-fat or nonfat sour cream
- ¼ cup green onion, sliced
- 2 tablespoons mint vinegar
- 1 green jalapeño pepper, cored and seeded
- ¼ cup unsweetened shredded coconut
- 1 fresh ginger, minced
- ½ teaspoon ground cumin seed

Combine all ingredients in a food processor and pulse until smooth but still somewhat coarse. Taste and adjust seasoning, adding salt, if desired. Refrigerate for several hours to allow flavors to blend. Serve at room temperature.

Fresh Green Chili and Cilantro Sambal

Yield: 1 cup

- 6 fresh green chili peppers, cored, seeded, and minced
- 1 cup fresh cilantro
- ¼ cup fresh garlic chives
- 1½ slices whole-wheat bread
- ¼ cup cilantro white wine vinegar
- ⅓ cup extra-virgin olive oil
- 1 tablespoon fresh ginger, minced
- ½ teaspoon ground cumin seed
- ½ teaspoon ground coriander seeds

In a food processor, combine all ingredients and pulse until smooth but still coarse. Season with salt, if desired. Refrigerate for several hours to allow flavors to blend. Serve at room temperature.

GREEN TOMATO CHUTNEY

Yield: 4 half-pints

- 3 pounds green tomatoes, cored and chopped
- 1 pound sweet green peppers, cored, seeded, and chopped
- 1 pound apples, cored and chopped
- 1 pound onions, chopped
- 1 cup raisins
- 3 cloves garlic, minced
- 1 fresh red or green hot pepper, cored, seeded, and minced
- 1 pint tarragon vinegar
- 2 cups packed light brown sugar
- 1 tablespoon non-iodized salt
- 1 teaspoon ground cumin seeds
- 1 teaspoon ground coriander seeds
- 1 teaspoon mustard seeds
- ½ teaspoon ground nutmeg

Combine all ingredients in a heavy-bottomed, nonreactive pot. Bring to a boil, stirring constantly. Reduce heat to low and simmer for 45 minutes, stirring frequently. Follow the standard directions for the boiling-water method of preserving, page 125.

MINT CHUTNEY

Yield: 8 half-pints

- 4 cup fresh spearmint, minced
- 1 cup fresh parsley, minced
- 4 cups apples, cored and chopped
- 1½ cup onion, chopped
- ½ cup golden raisins
- ½ cup blanched almonds, chopped
- 2 cups packed light brown sugar
- 1 pint mint vinegar
- 1 tablespoon mustard seeds
- 1 teaspoon coriander seeds
- 1 teaspoon non-iodized salt

Combine all ingredients in a heavy-bottomed, nonreactive pot. Bring to a boil, stirring constantly. Reduce heat to low, simmer 20 minutes, stirring frequently. Follow the directions for the boiling-water method of preserving, page 125.

Dried Apricot Chutney

Yield: 4 half-pints

- 1 pound dried apricots, chopped
- 1 pound onions, chopped
- 1 cup golden raisins
- ½ cup pine nuts
- 1 fresh red or green hot pepper, seeded and minced
- 3 cloves garlic, minced
- ½ cup orange juice
- Zest of 2 oranges
- Zest of 1 lemon
- 2 tablespoons fresh ginger, minced
- 1½ cups orange mint white wine vinegar
- 1½ cups packed light brown sugar
- 2 teaspoons non-iodized salt
- 1 teaspoon mustard seeds
- 1 teaspoon ground cardamom seeds
- ½ teaspoon ground cinnamon
- ½ teaspoon ground allspice

Combine all ingredients in a heavy-bottomed, nonreactive pot. Bring to boil, stirring constantly. Reduce heat to low and simmer for 45 minutes, stirring frequently. Follow the standard directions for the boiling-water method of preserving, page 125.

Mango Chutney

Yield: 4 half-pints

- 4 cups mango, peeled, seeded, and chopped
- 1 pound onions, chopped
- 1 cup golden raisins
- 2 limes, seeded and chopped
- ½ cup blanched almonds, chopped
- ½ cup fresh ginger, minced
- 2 cloves garlic, minced
- 1 fresh red or green hot pepper, cored, seeded, and minced

2 cups packed light brown sugar

1 cup cilantro white wine vinegar

¼ cup orange juice

¼ cup lemon juice

2 tablespoons fresh orange zest

2 teaspoons non-iodized salt

1 tablespoon mustard seeds

½ teaspoon ground cloves

½ teaspoon ground cinnamon

½ teaspoon turmeric

Combine all ingredients in a heavy-bottomed, nonreactive pot. Bring to a boil, stirring constantly. Reduce heat to low and simmer for 45 minutes, stirring frequently. Follow the standard directions for the boiling-water method of preserving, page 125.

APPLE-LOVAGE CHUTNEY

Yield: 6 half-pints

6 cups apples, cored and chopped

1 cup fresh lovage, minced

1 medium sweet red pepper, cored, seeded, and chopped

1 medium red tomato, cored, peeled, and chopped

1 medium green tomato, cored and chopped

½ pound onion, chopped

3 cloves garlic, minced

1 cup golden raisins

¼ cup fresh ginger, minced

1½ cups packed light brown sugar

1 cup lovage white wine vinegar

1 tablespoon mustard seeds

1 teaspoon celery seeds

Combine all ingredients in a heavy-bottomed, nonreactive pot. Bring to a boil, stirring constantly. Reduce heat to low and simmer for 30 minutes, stirring frequently. Follow the standard directions for the boiling-water method of preserving, page 125.

Variation. Substitute fresh spearmint and mint vinegar for the lovage and vinegar.

Rhubarb Chutney

Yield: 6 half-pints

- 6 cups rhubarb, chopped
- 1 cup red onion, chopped
- 1 cup apple, cored and chopped
- 1 cup dried cherries
- 3 cloves garlic, minced
- 1 tablespoon fresh ginger, minced
- ½ cup fresh lovage, minced
- 2 cups packed light brown sugar
- 1 cup spice red wine vinegar
- 1 teaspoon ground cinnamon
- 1 teaspoon ground cloves
- 1 teaspoon ground allspice
- 1 teaspoon ground coriander seeds

Combine all ingredients in a heavy-bottomed, nonreactive pot. Bring to a boil, stirring constantly. Reduce heat to low and simmer for 30 minutes, stirring frequently. Follow the standard directions for the boiling-water method of preserving, page 125.

Cranberry Chutney

Yield: 8 half-pints

- 6 cups fresh cranberies
- 2 medium navel oranges, rind grated, pith discarded, and the fruit coarsely chopped
- 2 cups apples, cored and chopped
- 1 cup onion, chopped
- 1 cup raisins
- 1 cup pecans, chopped
- 1 cup orange juice
- 1 clove garlic, minced
- 2 cups packed light brown sugar
- ½ cup tarragon or hyssop vinegar
- ¼ cup fresh tarragon or hyssop, minced
- ½ teaspoon ground ginger
- ½ teaspoon ground cloves
- ½ teaspoon ground allspice
- ½ teaspoon ground cinnamon

Combine all ingredients in a heavy-bottomed, nonreactive pot. Bring to a boil, stirring constantly. Reduce heat to low and simmer for 20 minutes, stirring frequently. Follow the standard directions for the boiling-water method of preserving, page 125.

Peach-Plum Chutney

Yield: 6 half-pints

- 1½ pounds peaches, pitted and chopped
- 1½ pounds yellow plums, pitted and chopped
- 1 cup onion, chopped
- 1 yellow sweet pepper, cored, seeded, and chopped
- 2 tablespoons fresh ginger, minced
- 1 clove garlic, minced
- 1 fresh green or red hot pepper, seeded and minced
- 2 cups packed light brown sugar
- 1 cup cinnamon basil white wine vinegar
- ½ cup fresh cinnamon basil, minced
- 1 tablespoon fresh lemon zest
- 1 teaspoon mustard seeds
- 1 teaspoon ground cloves
- 1 teaspoon ground cinnamon
- ½ teaspoon ground coriander seeds
- ½ teaspoon turmeric
- 2 teaspoons non-iodized salt

Combine all ingredients in a heavy-bottomed, nonreactive pot. Bring to a boil, stirring constantly. Reduce heat to low and simmer for 20 minutes, stirring frequently. Follow the standard directions for the boiling-water method of preserving, page 125.

Apple (or Pear) Chutney

Yield: 8 half-pints

8	cups apples or pears, cored and chopped
1	lemon, chopped and seeded
1	cup golden raisins
1	cup onion, chopped
1	cup walnuts, chopped
2	cloves garlic, minced
1½	cups packed light brown sugar
1½	cups hyssop apple cider or malt vinegar
2	fresh green or red hot peppers, cored, seeded, and minced
3	tablespoons fresh hyssop, minced
1	tablespoon fresh ginger, minced
1	tablespoon mustard seeds
½	teaspoon ground cardamon seeds
½	teaspoon ground allspice

Combine all ingredients in a heavy-bottomed, nonreactive pot. Bring to a boil, stirring constantly. Reduce heat to low and simmer for 30 minutes, stirring frequently. Follow the standard directions for the boiling-water method of preserving, page 125.

Jellies, Jams, and Preserves

Herb Jelly

Herb jellies make wonderful fillings for tea sandwiches, combining well with sweet butter or fresh goat cheese or cream cheese. They also complement roasted or grilled meats. Of course, herb jellies are delightful with biscuits, breads, and muffins, even peanut butter sandwiches!

Use just one herb or a combination. Don't forget to consider herb flowers like roses or lavender and root herbs like ginger and horseradish.

Yield: 4 to 5 half-pints

- 1-2 cups chopped herb leaves, flowers, or roots (depending on the intensity of the herb and the desired flavor), or ⅓ cup herb seeds
- 1½ cups boiling water
- ½ cup vinegar (choose one flavored with the same herb or one that is complementary)
- 3½ cups sugar
- 3 ounces liquid fruit pectin

Place the herbs in a bowl. Pour boiling water over the top. Cover and let steep for 30 minutes. Strain and measure liquid, adding water, if necessary, to yield 1½ cups.

Pour the herb liquid into a large, heavy nonreactive kettle. Stir in the vinegar and sugar. Place over high heat and cook, stirring, until the mixture comes to a full rolling boil. Stir in the pectin. Continue cooking and stirring until mixture reaches a hard boil that can't be stirred down. Cook for 1 more minute.

Skim off any foam from the surface, then ladle into hot sterilized half-pint canning jars, leaving ¼-inch headspace. Wipe the rims and attach two-piece canning lids or seal with paraffin. If using canning lids, follow the standard directions for boiling-water method of preserving, page 125, boiling for five minutes.

Wine Jelly

Use the best-quality fortified wine possible for these jellies, matching them to a vinegar. They are a flavorful relish to main courses as well as delightful with breads and muffins. Melted, they make a splendid glaze for fruit tarts. They can also be made with regular table wine, but the flavor is not as intense.

Yield: 5 to 6 half-pints

- ¾ cup water
- ⅓ cup sherry, port, or other matching vinegar, preferably one flavored with herbs
- 8 herb sprigs of the same herbs that flavor the vinegar, tied together with kitchen cord

    One 1¾-ounce powdered regular pectin
- 2½ cups cream sherry, port, or other fortified wine
- 4½ cups sugar

Combine the water, vinegar, and herbs in a large, heavy nonreactive kettle. Place over medium heat and bring to a boil. Remove from heat, cover, and let steep for 30 minutes. Remove herbs. Stir in the powdered pectin, mixing it in well. Place over medium-high heat and, stirring constantly, bring to a boil that can't be stirred down. Continue boiling for 1 minute. Stir in the wine and sugar. Reduce the heat to low and continue cooking until sugar is dissolved, or about 3 minutes. Skim off any foam from the surface, then ladle into hot sterilized half-pint canning jars, leaving ¼-inch headspace. Wipe the rims and attach two-piece canning lids or seal with paraffin. If using canning lids, follow the standard directions for boiling-water method of preserving, page 125, boiling for five minutes.

Fruit Juice-Herb Jelly

Most health-food stores carry a large selection of fruit juices sweetened with grape juice. These offer an easy way to make a wide range of unusual jellies flavored with herbs.

Yield: 4 to 5 half-pints

- 2½ cups fruit juice
- 1 cup fresh herbs
- 4 cups sugar
- ¼ cup vinegar
- 3 ounces liquid pectin

In a heavy nonreactive saucepan, bring the fruit juice to a boil. Add the herbs, cover, and let steep for 30 minutes. Strain and combine fruit juice with sugar and vinegar in a large, heavy nonreactive kettle. Place over high heat and cook, stirring, until the mixture comes to a full rolling boil. Stir in pectin. Continue cooking and stirring until mixture reaches a hard boil that can't be stirred down. Cook for 1 more minute. Skim off any foam from the surface, then ladle into hot sterilized half-pint canning jars, leaving ¼-inch headspace. Wipe rims and attach two-piece canning lids or seal with paraffin. If using canning lids, follow standard directions for boiling-water method of preserving, page 125, boiling for 5 minutes.

Juice-Herb-Vinegar Combinations

Orange and cranberry juices, cranberry or rosemary vinegar and rosemary

Apple cider, sage cider vinegar, and sage

Apple juice, thyme white wine vinegar, and thyme

Cranberry juice, savory cranberry vinegar, and savory

Pineapple-orange juice, lemon thyme white wine vinegar, and lemon thyme

Pink grapefruit juice, tarragon white wine vinegar, and tarragon

Raspberry or apricot juice, rose geranium white wine vinegar, and rose geranium

Orange juice, purple basil red wine vinegar, and purple basil

Cherry juice, lavender white wine vinegar, and lavender flowers

Peach juice, anise basil white wine vinegar, and anise basil

Strawberry juice, mint white wine vinegar, and mint

Tomato juice, basil white wine vinegar, and basil

Nectarine juice, cilantro rice vinegar, and cilantro

Note: Fresh apple juice, whether bought or homemade, contains enough natural pectin to preclude the addition of commercial pectin. When using apple juice, omit the pectin and cook the jelly until it reaches 220° F on a candy thermometer.

Hot Pepper Jam

A southern favorite served with cream cheese and crackers, this spicy-sweet jam is also good with roasted or grilled meats, sandwiches, and vegetables.

Yield: 8 half-pints

4–6 sweet red peppers, cored and seeded
4–6 hot red peppers, cored and seeded
  2 cups cilantro or hot pepper red wine vinegar
  6 cups sugar
  6 ounces liquid pectin

In a food processor or blender, puree the two types of peppers separately until you have 1¾ cups of pureed sweet peppers and ½ cup hot peppers. In a large, heavy nonreactive kettle, combine the pureed peppers, vinegar, and sugar. Place over medium-high heat and, stirring constantly, cook until the sugar dissolves. Bring to a boil, continuing to stir, and boil for 4 minutes. Stir in pectin and bring to a rolling boil that can't be stirred down. Cook for 1 more minute. Skim off any foam from the surface, then ladle into hot sterilized half-pint canning jars, leaving ¼-inch headspace. Wipe the rims and attach two-piece canning lids or seal with paraffin. If using canning lids, Follow the standard directions for boiling-water method of preserving, page 125, boiling for five minutes.

Variation. Green sweet and hot peppers may be used instead of the red peppers.

Pear-Honey Preserves

Yield: 4 half-pints

  4 pounds pears, cored, peeled, and cut into 1-inch pieces
 ¾ cup hyssop or spice white wine vinegar
  1 cup honey
  2 teaspoons ground cinnamon
 ½ teaspoon ground cloves
 ½ teaspoon ground cardamom seeds
  1 cup pecans, chopped
 ⅔ cup dried currants

In a large, heavy nonreactive saucepan, combine the pears, vinegar, honey, cinnamon, cloves, and cardamom. Cook over medium heat, stirring frequently, until the mixture begins to boil. Reduce heat to low and simmer until thick, or a candy thermometer reaches 220° F, or about 40 minutes. Stir in the nuts and currants. Continue to simmer, partially covered and stirring occasionally, for 15 minutes. Follow the standard directions for boiling-water method of preserving, page 125.

BLUEBERRY PRESERVES

Yield: 4 or 5 half-pints

- 4 cups blueberries, fresh or frozen
- ¼ cup blueberry-spice white or red wine vinegar
- 1 cup packed light brown sugar
- ¼ teaspoon ground allspice
- ¼ teaspoon ground cinnamon
- ¼ teaspoon ground cloves

Combine all ingredients in a large, heavy nonreactive saucepan over medium-high heat until the mixture comes to a boil. Reduce heat to low and simmer until thick, or a candy thermometer reaches 220° F, or about 30 minutes. Follow the standard directions for boiling-water method of preserving, page 125.

STRAWBERRY-RHUBARB PRESERVES

Yield: 4 half-pints

- 4 cups strawberries, hulled and halved
- 4 cups rhubarb, cut in 1-inch pieces
- 4 cups sugar
- ½ cup lemon balm white wine or rice vinegar
- ⅓ cup orange juice
- 2 tablespoon fresh orange zest
- 1 cup walnuts, chopped

In a large, heavy nonreactive saucepan, combine the strawberries, rhubarb, sugar, vinegar, orange juice, and orange zest. Cook over medium heat, stirring frequently, until the mixture begins to boil. Reduce heat to low and simmer until thick, or a candy thermometer reaches 220° F, or about 40 minutes. Stir in the nuts. Continue to simmer, partially covered and stirring occasionally, for 2 minutes. Follow the standard directions for boiling-water method of preserving, page 125.

TOMATO PRESERVES

Yield: 3 half-pints

- 4 pounds plum tomatoes, peeled and cored
- 1½ cups packed light brown sugar
- 1½ cups sugar
- 1 cup water
- ½ cup cinnamon basil vinegar
- ¼ cup fresh ginger, minced
- 1 teaspoon ground cinnamon

Combine all ingredients in a large, heavy nonreactive saucepan. Bring to a boil over medium-high heat, stirring frequently. Reduce heat to low and simmer until thick, about 1 hour, stirring frequently. Follow the standard directions for boiling-water method of preserving, page 125.

DESSERTS AND SWEETS

VINEGAR PIE I

Yield: 1 pie

One 9-inch pie shell, unbaked

4 large eggs

¾ cup sugar

¼ cup honey

¼ cup flavored vinegar

3 tablespoons unbleached all-purpose flour

6 tablespoons unsalted butter, melted and cooled

Preheat oven to 450° F. Line the chilled pie shell with parchment, then put in beans, rice, or pie weights. Bake for 10 minutes, then remove the weights and paper. Return the pie shell to the oven and reduce heat to 350° F. Bake for 8 to 10 minutes, or until just golden. Remove from oven and let it cool.

In a bowl, beat the eggs until smooth and lemon-yellow. Add the sugar, honey, vinegar, and flour and beat well, then mix in the butter. Pour into the baked pie shell. Bake at 350° F for 25 minutes, or until the filling is set. Let cool before serving. Serve with lightly sweetened, freshly whipped cream, or, if using a fruit vinegar, with some fresh fruit cut into pieces and lightly sweetened.

VINEGAR PIE

Vinegar pie is a throwback to times when fresh fruit and flavorings were not readily available. It utilizes those staples of the farm larder — butter, sugar, and eggs. Basically these are chess pies with vinegar as flavoring. There are a number of different variations, depending on the region. Experiment with different vinegars, including those flavored with spices, flowers, fruits, and "sweet" herbs, such as angelica, sweet cicely, and mint.

Vinegar Pie II

Yield: 1 pie

>One 9-inch pie shell, unbaked
2 large egg yolks
1 large egg
½ cup sugar
2 tablespoons unbleached all-purpose flour
¼ cup plus 2 teaspoons flavored vinegar
½ cup unsalted butter, melted and cooled
2 egg whites
2 tablespoons sugar

Prepare the pie shell as in Variation I. After the shell has been baked, increase the temperature to 450°F. In a bowl, beat the egg yolks and whole egg until foamy, then add the sugar and flour a little at a time, mixing after each addition. Add the ¼ cup vinegar and butter, blending well. Pour into the prebaked pie shell and bake for 10 minutes, then reduce the heat to 350°F. Bake for another 20 minutes, or until the filling is set.

In a bowl, beat the egg whites until they hold soft peaks, then add sugar a teaspoon at a time, beating until stiff peaks form. Beat in the 2 teaspoons vinegar. Spread this meringue over the filling and bake on the top rack in the oven at 350°F for 10 minutes, or until the meringue is set and golden. Cool before serving.

Vinegar Pie III

Yield: 1 pie

>One 9-inch pie shell, unbaked
½ cup butter, at room temperature
1 cup sugar
4 large eggs, separated
1 cup half-and-half cream
3 tablespoons flavored vinegar
Salt

Prepare the pie shell as in Variation I, then increase oven temperature to 450° F. In a bowl, cream butter and sugar until fluffy. Beat in egg yolks one at a time, beating well. Add cream and vinegar in a thin stream, blending well. In another bowl, beat egg whites with a pinch of salt until stiff peaks form. Fold one-fourth of whites into yolk mixture. Fold this into remaining whites and pour filling into baked pie shell. Bake for 15 minutes, then reduce heat to 350°F and bake for 25 minutes, or until filling is set. Cool before serving.

Vinegar Pie IV

Yield: 1 pie

  4 large eggs
  1 cup sugar
  4 tablespoons butter, melted and cooled
  3 tablespoons rose petal vinegar
  1 cup heavy cream, whipped to stiff peaks
  ¼ cup blanched, slivered almonds, toasted

Prepare the pie shell as in Variation I. In a bowl, beat eggs until foamy. Add sugar, butter, and vinegar, and mix well. Pour into baked pie shell. Bake for 35 minutes, or until filling is set. Let cool completely. Spread whipped cream over pie, then sprinkle with almonds. Chill until ready to serve.

Vegetarian Mincemeat

Yield: 5 pints

  1 orange
  1 lemon
  3 pounds apples, cored and finely chopped
  3 pounds pears, cored and finely chopped
  1 cup walnuts, finely chopped
  ½ cup golden raisins
  ½ cup dried currants
  ½ cup dried cranberries or cherries
  2 cups packed light brown sugar
  ½ cup mixed-spice apple cider or sherry vinegar
  ½ cup apple brandy or dry sherry
  1 teaspoon ground cinnamon
  1 teaspoon ground nutmeg
  1 teaspoon ground ginger
  1 teaspoon ground allspice
  1 teaspoon ground cloves

Peel the zest from the orange and lemon and set aside. Peel off the inner white rind and throw away. Chop the remaining fruit. In a heavy nonreactive pot, combine the citrus zest and fruit with the remaining ingredients. Place over medium-low heat and cook, stirring, until the sugar is dissolved. Bring the mixture to a simmer and cook, stirring occasionally, for 45 minutes to 1 hour, or until thick. Use immediately, freeze in pint containers, or follow the standard directions for boiling-water method of preserving, page 125.

Vinegar Candy (taffy, hard candy, or sponge candy)

The same combination of ingredients in this recipe will yield different results, depending on how long it is cooked. A different texture is achieved with the addition of baking soda. Experiment with different kinds of vinegar and other flavorings, including herbs, flowers, and spices.

Yield: 1 pound

- 2 cups sugar or 1 cup sugar and 1 cup light corn syrup, sorghum molasses, or honey
- ½ cup herb or other flavored vinegar
- 2 tablespoons butter
- 1 teaspoon flavoring extract, such as herb, fruit, or spice (optional)

  Food coloring (optional)

In a heavy nonreactive saucepan, combine sugar, vinegar, and butter. Cook over low heat, stirring until sugar is dissolved. If sugar crystals form on the side of the pan, either cover the pan for several minutes to allow steam to dissolve them or use a moistened pastry brush to wipe down the sides of the pan. Increase heat to medium.

To make taffy, bring to a rolling boil and cook without stirring until a candy thermometer reads 265° F. Remove from heat and stir in flavoring and coloring, if desired. Pour onto a marble surface or buttered plate and let cool. Sprinkle a work surface, such as marble, with confectioner's sugar and butter a pair of kitchen scissors. When the candy is cool enough to hold a dent when pressing with a finger, butter your fingers and gather the candy into a ball. Pull the candy, using both hands to stretch it about 18 inches, then fold it over on itself. Repeat until the candy is a shiny, gleaming ribbon. Stretch it into thin rope, then cut into 1-inch pieces and drop onto sugared surface. Store in a tightly covered container.

To make hard candy drops, bring to a rolling boil and cook without stirring until a candy thermometer reads 300° F. Remove from heat and stir in flavoring and coloring, if desired. Drop spoonfuls of the mixture onto a very lightly greased or nonstick baking sheet on an absolutely flat work surface. Let cool until hard, or about 30 minutes. Gently remove from the baking sheet. Wrap candy in plastic wrap or place in an airtight container with pieces not touching and with wax paper between the layers.

To make sponge candy, bring to a rolling boil and cook without stirring until a candy thermometer reads 300° F. Remove from heat and stir in flavoring and coloring, if desired, then 1 tablespoon of baking soda. Pour into a well-buttered 9-inch-square baking pan. When cool, break into pieces with a large knife handle. Store in an airtight container.

Sweet-and-Sour Jellies

Yield: 1¼ pounds

- 2 cups sugar
- 3 envelopes unflavored gelatin
- ½ cup water
- ¾ cup herb or other flavored vinegar
- 2 tablespoons minced fresh herbs, flowers, or citrus zest, or ½ teaspoon ground spices

  Extra-fine granulated sugar, purchased or made in a food processor

Using a heavy nonreactive saucepan, combine the sugar, gelatin, and water. Over medium heat, bring the mixture to a boil, stirring constantly. Boil for 15 minutes or longer, until the mixture forms a filament several inches long when poured from a spoon. Remove from heat. Stir in the vinegar and herbs or other flavoring. Pour into a 9-by-5-inch loaf pan rinsed with cold water. Let stand until very firm, or at least 4 hours. Go around the edges of the pan with a moistened table knife. Place a baking sheet over the pan, and holding the two together, invert the loaf pan. With a serrated knife dipped in cold water, cut the candy into 1-inch cubes. Spread the pieces on a baking sheet or other flat surface and sift extra-fine sugar over them, rolling to coat all sides. Place jellies on a cake rack, cover with a cloth, and allow to dry for several hours. Store in a cardboard box or paper bag.

Vinegar Ice

This ice can take many forms, depending on the vinegar used. Made with lavender or rose vinegar, it is a fitting finale for an elegant luncheon. Vinegar flavored with anise hyssop or cinnamon basil yields an ice perfect for a palate freshener between courses of a meal. Adding chopped fresh herbs or flowers intensifies the flavor.

Yield: 1 quart

- 2 large egg whites
- 2¼ cups sugar
- 1 cup water
- 1½ cups flavored vinegar

In a large nonreactive bowl, beat egg whites until stiff; set aside. Combine sugar and water in a medium saucepan and cook over high heat, stirring constantly, until sugar dissolves and mixture reaches a full, rolling boil. Remove from heat and pour in a thin stream over egg whites, whisking constantly. Continue whisking and slowly add vinegar. Cover and chill thoroughly. Transfer to ice cream machine and freeze according to manufacturer's directions.

Herb Tea Sorbet

Utilize the wide variety of herbal tea mixtures available at grocery and health food stores, matching the vinegar to the dominant flavor in the tea. For example, there are great mint tea blends that would naturally pair with a mint vinegar.

Yield: 1 quart

- 1 quart boiling water
- 4 herbal tea bags
- ½ cup sugar
- ¼ cup flavored vinegar

Pour the boiling water over the tea bags in a nonreactive heatproof container. Let steep for 15 minutes. Remove the tea bags and stir in the sugar and vinegar, stirring until the sugar is dissolved. Chill thoroughly. Transfer to an ice cream machine and freeze according to the manufacturer's directions.

Rose-Zucchini Cake

Yield: One 10-inch bundt or tube cake

- 1 cup butter, at room temperature
- 2 cups sugar
- 4 large eggs
- 1½ cups zucchini, shredded
- 2 tablespoons fresh rose geranium leaves, minced
- 2 tablespoons fresh rose petals, minced
- 3 cups unbleached all-purpose flour
- 1½ teaspoons baking soda
- 1½ teaspoons ground cardamom seeds
- 1 teaspoon salt
- ¼ cup buttermilk
- ⅓ cup rose petal or rose geranium vinegar
- 1 cup pecans, chopped and lightly dusted with flour

Preheat oven to 350° F. Grease and flour a 10-inch bundt or tube pan. In a bowl, cream butter and sugar until light and fluffy. Add eggs one at a time, beating well after each one. Mix in zucchini, rose geranium leaves, and rose petals. In another bowl combine flour, baking soda, cardamom, and salt. Alternately add flour mixture and the buttermilk and vinegar to the creamed mixture, beating well after each addition. Stir in nuts. Pour into prepared pan and bake 1 hour, or until a toothpick inserted comes out clean. Cool 10 minutes in pan, then invert onto a cooling rack.

SPICE CAKE

Yield: One 9-inch-square cake

- 1½ cups sugar
- ½ cup canola oil
- 2 large eggs
- ¾ cup skim milk
- ¼ cup spice vinegar
- 2 cups unbleached all-purpose flour
- 1 teaspoon baking soda
- 1 teaspoon ground cinnamon
- 1 teaspoon ground cloves
- 1 teaspoon ground allspice
- 1 teaspoon ground nutmeg
- 1 teaspoon ground coriander seeds
- ½ teaspoon salt
- ½ cup raisins or dried currants, cranberries, or cherries, lightly dusted with flour
- ½ cup walnuts, chopped, lightly dust with flour

Preheat oven to 350° F. Grease and flour a 9-inch-square baking pan. In a bowl, beat sugar and oil until light and creamy. Add eggs, milk, and vinegar and mix well. In another bowl combine flour, baking soda, cinnamon, cloves, allspice, nutmeg, coriander, and salt. Set aside ¼ cup and combine with dried fruit and nuts to coat. Stir dry ingredients into creamed mixture. Fold in dried fruit and nuts. Pour into prepared pan. Bake for 1 hour, or until a toothpick inserted in the middle comes out clean. Serve warm.

. . . .

V I N E G A R
▼
*made especially
for you by*

. . . .

. . . .

V I N E G A R
▼
*made especially
for you by*

. . . .

. . . .

V I N E G A R
▼
*made especially
for you by*

. . . .

. . . .

V I N E G A R
▼
*made especially
for you by*

. . . .

. . . .

V I N E G A R
▼
*made especially
for you by*

. . . .

SOURCES FOR
HERB PLANTS AND SEEDS

W. Atlee Burpee & Company
300 Park Avenue
Warminster, PA 18974
(800) 888-1447

Carroll Gardens
P.O. Box 310
Westminster, MD 21158
(410) 848-5422
Catalog, $3

Chili Pepper Emporium
P.O. Box 7397
Albuquerque, NM 87194
(505) 242-7538
Free catalog

Circle Herb Farm
Route 1, Box 247
East Jordan, MI 49727
(616) 536-2729

Companion Plants
7247 North Coolville Ridge Road
Athens, OH 45701
(614) 592-4643
Catalog, $2

The Cook's Garden
P.O. Box 535
Londonderry, VT 05148
(802) 824-3400
Catalog, $1

Country Heritage Nurseries
P.O. Box 536
Hartford, MI 49057
(616) 621-2491
Free catalog

DeGiorgi Seed Company
6011 N Street
Omaha, NE 68117
(402) 731-3901
Catalog, $2

Filaree Farm
Route 2, Box 162
Okanogan, WA 98840
(509) 422-6940
Catalog, $2

The Flowery Branch Seed Co.
P.O. Box 1330
Flowery Branch, GA 30542
(404) 536-8380
Catalog, $2

Forest Farm
990 Tetherow Road
Williams, OR 97544-9599
(503) 846-7269
Catalog, $3

Fox Hill Farm
P.O. Box 9
Parma, MI 49269-0009
(517) 531-3179
Catalog, $1

Fragrant Fields
128 Front Street
Dongola, IL 62926
(618) 827-3677
Free catalog

The Gathered Herb
   & Greenhouse
12114 North State Road
Otisville, MI 48463
(810) 631-6572
Catalog, $2

Glade Valley Nursery
9226 Links Road
Walkersville, MD 21793
(301) 845-8145
Catalog, $2

Goodwin Creek Gardens
P.O. Box 83
Williams, OR 97544
(503) 488-3308
Catalog, $1

The Gourmet Gardener
8650 West College Boulevard
Overland Park, KS 66210
(913) 345-0490
*Catalog, $2 (refundable with
   order)*

Hartman's Herb Farm
Old Dana Road
Barre, MA 01005
(508) 355-2015
Catalog, $2

Havasu Hills Herb Farm
20150 Rough & Ready Trail
Sonora, CA 95370
(209) 536-1420
Catalog, $1

Heirloom Garden Seeds
P.O. Box 138
Guerneville, CA 95446
(707) 869-0967
Catalog, $2.50

The Herbfarm
32804 Issaquah-Fall City Road
Fall City, WA 98024
(206) 222-7103
Catalog, $3.50

Herbs-Liscious
1702 South Sixth Street
Marshalltown, IA 50158
(515) 752-4976
*Catalog, $2 (refundable with first
   order)*

The Hollow, Orchids & Herbs
71 German Crossroad
Ithaca, NY 14850
(607) 277-3380

Hortico, Inc.
723 Robson Road
Waterdown, ON
Canada L0R 2H1
(905) 689-6984
Catalog, $3

It's About Thyme
11726 Manchaca Road
Austin, TX 78748
(512) 280-1192
Catalog, $1

Johnny's Selected Seeds
Foss Hill Road
Albion, ME 04910
(207) 437-9294
Free catalog

Krystal Wharf Farms
RD 2, P.O. Box 2112
Mansfield, PA 16933
(717) 549-8194
fax (717) 549-5194
Free catalog

Legacy Herbs
HC 70, P.O. Box 442
Mountain View, AR 72560
(501) 269-4051
Catalog, $.50

Le Jardin du Gourmet
P.O. Box 275
St. Johnsbury Center, VT 05863
(802) 748-1446
Catalog, $.50

Lewis Mountain Herbs &
   Everlastings
2345 Street, Route 247
Manchester, OH 45144
(513) 549-2484
Free catalog

Lily of the Valley Herb Farm
3969 Fox Avenue
Minerva, OH 44657
(216) 862-3920
*Catalog, $2 (refundable with
   order)*

Logee's Greenhouses
141 North Street
Danielson, CT 06239
(203) 774-8038
Catalog, $3

McClure & Zimmerman
P.O. Box 368
Friesland, WI 53935-0368
(414) 326-4220
Free catalog

Merry Gardens
P.O. Box 595
Camden, ME 04843-0595
(207) 236-9064
Catalog, $2

Native Seeds/SEARCH
2509 North Campbell, #325
Tucson, AZ 85719
(602) 327-9123
Catalog, $1

The Natural Gardening Company
217 San Anselmo Avenue
San Anselmo, CA 94960
(415) 456-5060
Free catalog

Nichols Garden Nursery
1190 North Pacific Highway
Albany, OR 97321-4598
(503) 928-9280

Park Seed Company
Cokesbury Road,
   Highway 254 N.
Greenwood, SC 29647-0001
(803) 223-8555
Free catalog

Pinetree Garden Seeds
Route 100, Box 300
New Gloucester, ME 04260
(207) 926-3400
Free catalog

Plants of the Southwest
Agua Fria, Route 6, Box 11-A
Santa Fe, NM 87505
(505) 471-2212
Catalog, $3.50

Rasland Herb Farm
NC 82 at US 13
Godwin, NC 28344-9712
(910) 567-2705
Catalog, $2.50

Redwood City Seed Company
P.O. Box 361
Redwood City, CA 94064
(415) 325-7333
Catalog, $1

Rabbit Shadow Farm
2880 East Highway 402
Loveland, CO 80537
(303) 667-5531
Free catalog

Richters
P.O. Box 26
Goodwood, ON
Canada L0C 1A0
(905) 640-6677
Catalog, $2

The Rosemary House
120 South Market Street
Mechanicsburg, PA 17055
(717) 697-5111
Catalog, $2

St. John's Herb Garden
7711 Hillmeade Road
Bowie, MD 20720
(301) 262-5302
Catalog, $5

Sandy Mush Herb Nursery
316 Surrett Cove Road
Leicester, NC 28748-9622
(704) 683-2014
Catalog, $4

Seeds Blum
Idaho City Stage
Boise, ID 83706
(208) 342-0858
Catalog, $3

Shepherd's Garden Seeds
6116 Highway 9
Felton, CA 95018
408-335-6910
Catalog, $1

Southern Exposure Seed
   Exchange
P.O. Box 170
Earlysville, VA 22936
(804) 973-4703
Catalog, $2

Stokes Seeds
P.O. Box 548
Buffalo, NY 14240
(716) 695-6980
Free catalog

Stokes Seeds
Box 10
St. Catharine's, ON
Canada L2R 6R6
(905) 688-4300

Sunnybrook Farms Nursery
9448 Mayfield Road
Chesterland, OH 44026
(216) 729-7232
*Catalog, $2 (refundable with
   order)*

Taylor's Herb Gardens
1535 Lone Oak Road
Vista, CA 92084
(619) 727-3485
Catalog, $3

Territorial Seed Company
P.O. Box 157
Cottage Grove, OR 97424
(503) 942-9547
Free catalog

Tinmouth Channel Farm
P.O. Box 428B, Town Highway 19
Tinmouth, VT 05773
(802) 446-2812
Catalog, $2

Triple Oaks Nursery
Route 47
Franklinville, NJ 08322
(609) 694-4272
Catalog, SASE

Vermont Bean Seed Company
Garden Lane
Fair Haven, VT 05743
(802) 273-3400
Free catalog

Washington National
    Cathedral Greenhouse
Wisconsin and Massachusetts
    Avenues
Washington, DC 20016-5098
(202) 537-6263
Brochure, $1

Wayside Gardens
1 Garden Lane
Hodges, SC 29695-0001
(800) 845-1124
Free catalog

Well-Sweep Herb Farm
317 Mt. Bethel Road
Port Murray, NJ 07865
(908) 852-5390
Catalog, $2

Westwind Seeds
2509 North Campbell, #139
Tucson, AZ 85719
(602) 888-3021

Wrenwood of Berkeley Springs
Route 4, Box 361
Berkeley Springs, WV 25411-9413
(304) 258-3071
Catalog, $2

SOURCES FOR VINEGAR,
VINEGAR-MAKING SUPPLIES,
BOTTLING, AND LABELING

Aspen TypoGraphix
1648 Old Hart Ranch Road
Roseville, CA 95661
(916) 786-5955
Labels

Balducci's
424 Sixth Avenue
New York, NY 10011
(212) 673-2600
Vinegars

Barrel Builders
P.O. Box 268
St. Helena, CA 94574
(707) 942-4291
Barrels

Chicama Vineyards
Stoney Hill Road, P.O. Box 430
West Tisbury, MA 02575-0430
(508) 693-0309
Vinegars

Corti Brothers
5770 Freeport Boulevard
Sacramento, CA 95822
(916) 736-3800
Vinegars

Dean & DeLuca
560 Broadway
New York, NY 10012
(212) 431-1691
Vinegars

The Herbarium
P.O. Box 246836
Sacramento, CA 95824
(916) 388-1582
Rubber stamps

Maison Glass
111 East 58th Street
New York, NY 10022
(212) 755-3316
Vinegars

Paprika Weiss Importer
1572 Second Avenue
New York, NY 10028
(212) 288-6117
Vinegars

Rafal Spice Company
2521 Russell Street
Detroit, MI 48207
(313) 259-6373
Containers, labels

G. B. Ratto & Co.
821 Washington Street
Oakland, CA 94607
(510) 832-6503
Vinegars

The Stamp Connection
20125 Colonel Glenn
Little Rock, AR 72210
(501) 821-3833
Catalog, $3
Rubber stamps

Sur La Table
84 Pine Street
Seattle, WA 98101
(206) 448-2244
Bottles

Sweet Antiques Gallery
P.O. Box 563
131 S. Main Street
Barre, VT 05641
(802) 479-3645
Bottles

Zabar's
2245 West 80th Street
New York, NY 10024
(212) 787-2000
Vinegars

Alley, Lynn. *Cooking with Fresh Herbs.* Carlsbad, CA: Lynn Alley, 1992.

Andrews, Glenn. *Making Flavored Oils & Vinegars.* Pownal, VT: Storey Communications, 1989.

Barton, Barbara J. *Gardening By Mail: A Source Book.* Boston: Houghton Mifflin, 1990.

Beckett, Barbara. *Creating Gourmet Gifts.* North Sydney: Allen & Unwin Pty. Ltd., 1992.

Bonar, Ann. *The Macmillan Treasury of Herbs.* New York: Macmillan, 1985

Bremness, Lesley. *The Complete Book of Herbs.* New York: Viking Penguin, 1988.

Brown, Marion. *Pickles and Preserves.* New York: Avenel Books, 1960.

Choate, Judith. *Gourmet Preserves.* New York: Grove Weidenfeld, 1987.

Creber, Ann. *Vinegars.* Boston: Charles E. Tuttle Co., 1992.

Dieckmann, Jane Marsh. *Salad Dressings!* Freedom, CA: The Crossing Press, 1987.

Foster, Gertrude B., and Rosemary F. Louden. *Park's Success with Herbs.* Greenwood, SC: Geo. W. Park Seed Co., 1980.

Garden Way Publishing, eds. *Herbs: 1001 Garden Questions Answered.* Pownal, VT: Storey Communications, 1990.

Graybill, Nina, and Maxine Rapoport. *The Pasta Salad Book.* Washington, DC: Farragut Publishing Co., 1984

Greene, Bert. *The Grains Cookbook.* New York: Workman Publishing, 1988.

——. *Greene on Greens.* New York: Workman Publishing, 1984.

Gunst, Kathy. *Condiments.* New York: G. P. Putnam's Sons, 1984.

Hopley, Claire. *Making & Using Mustards.* Pownal, VT: Storey Communications, 1991.

Horn, Jane, ed. *Cooking A to Z.* San Ramon, CA: Chevron Chemical Company, 1988.

Hutson, Lucinda. *The Herb Garden Cookbook.* Austin, TX: Texas Monthly Press, 1987.

Johnson, Marsha Peters. *Gourmet Vinegars.* Lake Oswego, OR: Culinary Arts Ltd., 1989.

Jordan, Michele Anna. *The Good Cook's Book of Oil & Vinegar.* Reading, MA: Addison-Wesley Publishing Co., 1992.

Kowalchik, Claire, & William H. Hylton, eds. *Rodale's Illustrated Encyclopedia of Herbs.* Emmaus, PA: Rodale Press, 1987.

Lake, Mark, and Judy Ridgway. *Oils, Vinegars, & Seasonings.* New York: Simon & Schuster, 1989.

Lathrop, Norma Jean. *Herbs: How to Select, Grow and Enjoy.* Tucson: HP Books, 1981.

Lima, Patrick. *The Harrowsmith Illustrated Book of Herbs.* Camden East, Ontario: Camden House, 1986.

Man, Rosamond, and Robin Weir. *The Compleat Mustard.* London: Constable, 1988.

McRae, Bobbi A. *The Herb Companion Wishbook and Resource Guide.* Loveland, CO: Interweave Press, 1992.

Norman, Jill. *Oils, Vinegars & Seasonings.* New York: Bantam Books, 1992.

Ogden, Shepherd, and Ellen Ogden. *The Cook's Garden.* Emmaus, PA: Rodale Press, 1989.

Oster, Maggie. *Recipes from an American Herb Garden.* New York: Macmillan, 1993.

Plagemann, Catherine, and M. F. K. Fisher. *Fine Preserving.* Reading, MA: Aris Books/ Addison-Wesley, 1986.

Romanowski, Frank, and Gail Canon. *Making Vinegar at Home.* Northampton, MA: Beer and Winemaking Supplies, Sixth Printing, 1992.

Schmidt, R. Marilyn. *Flavored Vinegars.* Barnegat Light, NJ: Pine Barrens Press, 1988.

Scicolone, Michele. *The Antipasta Table.* New York: William Morrow and Co., 1991.

Shaudys, Phyllis. *Herbal Treasures.* Pownal, VT: Garden Way Publishing, 1990.

——. *The Pleasure of Herbs.* Pownal, VT: Garden Way Publishing, 1986.

Shepherd, Renee. *Recipes From A Kitchen Garden.* Felton, CA: Shepherd's Garden Publishing, 1987.

Shepherd, Renee, and Fran Raboff. *Recipes from a Kitchen Garden Vol. 2.* Felton, CA: Shepherd's Garden Publishing, 1991.

Shelton, Ferne. *Colonial Kitchen Herbs.* High Point, NC: Hutcraft, 1972.

Sinnes, A. Cort. *The Grilling Book.* Berkeley, CA: Aris Books, 1985.

Stancer, Claire. *The Ultimate Salad Dressing Book.* New York: McGraw-Hill Book Co., 1988.

Stobart, Tom. *Herbs, Spices and Flavourings.* New York: Viking Penguin, 1987.

Thorson Editorial Board. *The Complete Cider Vinegar.* Northamptonshire, England: Thorsons Publishers, Ltd., 1989.

Vainas, Ellen. *The Vinegar Book.* Lynn, MA: Brown Bag Books, 1981.

Walter, Eugene. *Hints & Pinches.* Atlanta: Longstreet Press, 1991.

Weitzel, Patricia, ed. *Herbs: A Cookbook and More.* Cleveland: The Western Reserve Herb Society, 1979.

Williamson, Donna. *More Simple Riches.* Harpers Ferry, WV: Sophie's Farm Publications, 1990.

Witty, Helen. *Fancy Pantry.* New York: Workman Publishing, 1986.

——. and Elizabeth Schneider Colchie. *Better Than Store-Bought.* New York: Harper & Row, 1979.

I N D E X